RELIGION
AND
SELF-ACCEPTANCE

RELIGION
AND
SELF-ACCEPTANCE

by

John F. Haught

PAULIST PRESS
New York/Paramus/Toronto

Library of Congress
Catalog Card Number: 75-44805

ISBN: 0-8091-1940-4

Published by Paulist Press
Editorial Office: 1865 Broadway, N.Y., N.Y. 10023
Business Office: 400 Sette Drive, Paramus, N.J. 07652

Printed and bound in the
United States of America

To my wife
Evelyn,
and my sons
Paul and Martin

M. 86

Preface

Although the title of the present work may not immediately suggest it, I have intended it to be, above all, an introductory essay in the philosophy of religion. As it turns out, the method I have employed requires more attention to the goal of self-acceptance than is usually given that concept. And since I see philosophy's purpose as self-appropriation, following Bernard Lonergan, I use the term self-acceptance as referring simultaneously to both philosophical and psychological interests. A great deal has been written on the relationship between religion and self-acceptance from both psychotherapeutic and theological points of view. But the philosopher of religion has traditionally avoided the theme of self-acceptance because it seemed peripheral to his concerns. This book attempts, in part at least, to compensate for that oversight and to reformulate the objectives of the philosophy of religion accordingly.

I must acknowledge at the outset my general indebtedness to the works especially of Bernard Lonergan, but also of Paul Ricoeur, Emerich Coreth, Paul Tillich and Henry Duméry. While I have attempted a fresh approach to the philosophical interrogation of religious life, and one with which these great thinkers might take issue at times, it is largely in response to their reflections that this book was written.

I would like to thank Georgetown University for the summer grant that facilitated the writing of this book. And in a very special way I thank my wife, Evelyn, for her advice, patience and the many hours spent typing the manuscript.

Introduction

One way of approaching the study of religious expressions and attitudes is to ask about their origin. For over a century now there has been an enormous amount of anthropological, psychological and historical inquiry into the origin of "religion." The prevailing assumption in much of it has been that if we can locate the source of religion we will be in a privileged position to criticize and evaluate the countless streams proliferating from it.

This method of investigation, however, has been severely challenged in recent years. To know the origin is not to know the essence of the phenomenon. To know the source is not to be in a position to evaluate, or validate or falsify definitively. Evolutionism and psychologism are guilty of the genetic fallacy. They assume that the entire substance of religious consciousness can be explained or explained away once we place a scholarly finger on its chronological or psychological point of departure.

Critiques of this genetic approach have come especially from the so-called phenomenologists of religion. These latter-day scholars insist that religion must be taken as a mode of consciousness *sui generis*. Any attempt to derive it from psychological drives, defense mechanisms, or sociological and cultural needs is apt to miss something essential to religious life. No matter how successful social scientists are in their quest, no matter how substantial their insights into the origin of so complex a phenomenon, apprehension of origin is not the whole story.

Phenomenology of religion seeks to understand religious life from the point of view of religious consciousness itself. As Eliade insists,

> . . . A religious phenomenon will only be recognized as such if it is grasped at its own level, that is to say, if it is studied *as* something religious. To try to grasp the essence of such a

1

phenomenon by means of physiology, sociology, economics, linguistics, art or any other study is false; it misses the one unique and irreducible element in it—the element of the sacred.[1]

The new science of religion tries to take religious man at his word, i.e., that his religion is a response to the "sacred." It puts in brackets the interesting question of how such religion comes into concrete awareness, how it may rely on psychic and cultural motives, etc. It also suspends methodologically any consideration of the question whether the affirmation of the sacred is a valid one. It is indifferent to the question whether religion is illusory or on sound epistemological soil. Instead phenomenology of religion, although a controversial and hard-to-isolate approach itself, is usually concerned with unfolding the structure of religious consciousness without regard to questions of value or validity. The results of its study have been unquestionably appreciable. Phenomenological approaches have helped to eradicate a great deal of methodological blundering. They have reinstated religious consciousness as irreducible to other modes of awareness. And they have forced scholars to deal fairly, without bias or unwarranted assumptions, with a most delicate subject.

Still the old questions linger. They are only artificially suppressed. The inquisitive man still regards the question of origin, value and validity essential to a full understanding of religious acts and attitudes. Phenomenological studies, important as they are, do not constitute a philosophy of religion. One cannot suspend critical questions indefinitely without doing violence to the inborn dynamics of the human mind. The question, "what gives rise to religious life?" may have been relativized by phenomenological studies, but it has not been, nor should it be, eradicated. And the question whether religious man is in touch with reality, whether his affirmation of the sacred is epistemologically integral, continues to surface in spite of the phenomenological reductions. Phenomenological studies have given us a needed breathing space. They have alerted us to the countless traps and devious presuppositions that accompany our asking questions about origin, value and validity. But on the whole they have summoned forth once again rather than eliminated our critical requirements. They have forced us to be more attentive to the *phenomenon* of religion. Precisely because of this they have given rise more vigorously than ever to questions for understanding and reflection. In short they have silently called for a revival of the philosophy of religion.

This book is a post-phenomenological reflection on man's attestation to the sacred. In particular it is addressed to the many forms of witnessing to a living God associated with Semitic religions and their Western derivatives. It is a critique respectful of the phenomenological movement. But it is also one which bows to the irrepressible injunctions of the mind that we be speculative, evaluative and critical as well as attentive toward given structures of religious life. The justification for this critical method will be provided in the first chapter.

We shall seek to reassociate questions of origin, value and validity with recent phenomenological studies of religious consciousness by asking how religious affirmations relate to a basic human desire, the desire to know. Such an approach will allow us to bring together, without dissolving their differences, the concerns of the philosopher and the social scientist. By asking about the relationship of religion to human desire we are led to such investigations as the following: What is the connection between religion and psychic needs? Can religious consciousness be critically grounded by positing its source as the will to meaning? What is the meaning of the language of belief in terms of the desire to know? And finally, how can the desire to know the real coexist with the perennial urge by men to saturate their social and psychic life with religious myths and stories?

Focusing on the desire to know allows us to revive in a chastened but still productive manner the question whence originates religious life. If response to the sacred does not somehow appear to arise from the "pure" desire to know, then its source is inevitably going to be located by social scientists in some other, perhaps infantile, psychic or social orientation. Unless religion is rooted in the desire to know, the validity of its formal testimony to the sacred or to "God" comes under challenge. Questions of origin, value and validity converge when we ask about the relationship of religion to what every intelligent person can identify in himself as

an ineradicable, dynamic desire to know. The following chapters
are an invitation to each reader to compose a personal critique of
religion by becoming increasingly awakened to his own desire to
know and asking how his or others' religious expressions conform
to or deviate from its demands.

In this book I shall not attempt to construct *ab initio* any
image or notion of God or the sacred. I shall simply take note of
the fact that God-language, religious acts and representations of
many types are part of the data of my experience. All of us have
been exposed in one way or another to the multiple manifestations
of religious life. I cannot avoid attending to these data and asking
questions about them. But I want to make certain that I am asking
the right questions. I think it is the task of a philosophy of religion
simply to ask whether and how various religious acts promote the
interests of the desire to know. The only commitment (but also the
most difficult) that the philosopher has to make is to the spontaneous precepts of this desire.

I do not think that any philosophy of religion should be in the
business of generating from within itself a concept of God or of
immanently construing the lineaments of the sacred. "Philosophy," Paul Ricoeur says, "does not start anything independently: supported by the non-philosophical, it derives its existence from
the substance of what has already been understood prior to reflection."[2] And Henri Duméry concurs:

> The philosopher, first of all, must be aware that his discipline
> is only a reflective technique applied to lived experience. He
> does not supplant the concrete subject, the thinking and acting
> man. Only the latter is really engaged and brings values into
> play. Only he does a free act; only he effectively conforms the
> means at his disposal to the end he pursues. The philosopher
> is always dependent upon the man and remains his pupil. He
> must clarify man, but not substitute himself for man. This is
> to say that philosophy always comes after life; it is a recovery
> of life; but it cannot be identified with life. Philosophy is, if
> you like, the word of life, it is not life itself.[3]

In a special way the philosophy of religion must take as its point of departure already existing pre-theoretical religious acts and language. Otherwise it ends up fabricating an abstract notion of the sacred or a "God of the philosophers" that has little relation to the vital flow of religious life. It is in the spirit of Duméry's and Ricoeur's conception of philosophical reflection that this book is written.

> Criticism begins from life and returns to life. It is only a reflective detour, the time of methodical judgment. It never suppresses that which nourishes it.[4]

> . . . we are in every way children of criticism, and we seek to go beyond criticism by means of criticism, by a criticism that is no longer reductive but restorative.[5]

> Beyond the desert of criticism, we wish to be called again.[6]

Finally, a theme that will dominate our inquiry and serve to pull together its various threads is that of self-acceptance. Treatments of the issue of knowledge and belief are usually undertaken without reference to this notion and ideal. In these pages, however, I shall attempt to show that the epistemological and psychological points of view must both strive toward the objective of self-acceptance. The experiment in cognitional self-awareness upon which this essay will be erected is not a mere intellectual exercise. My underlying intention throughout is to have the reader participate in the struggle toward self-acceptance that psychotherapy most explicitly idealizes. Ultimately one of the crucial and most vitally critical tests of the genuineness of a religious stance is whether or not it promotes this ideal. Self-acceptance is perhaps the basic criterion not only of mental health but also of epistemic integrity. An animating acceptance of oneself *as a knower* requires the same courage that the psychotherapist or existentialist philosopher associate with self-acceptance. Without such courage the self that one accepts is a restricted one, and the knower that one envisions himself to be is a mere looker, classifier, deducer, computer, etc., but not a knower in possession of himself. We shall be especially interested in the relationship of religious life and faith to this goal of self-appropriation as a knower. In what ways does religion promote or frustrate the process toward self-knowledge?

The problem of belief is inseparable from the problem of self-acceptance. But traditional treatises in the philosophy of religion have scarcely recognized this. Justifications or refutations of belief have been carried out as though epistemological interests are separable from the matter of personal or psychic wholeness. Our approach, on the contrary, will make self-appropriation the integrating principle in both epistemological and psychological questions about religious life, language and belief. In this way we may see the philosophy of religion as part of the larger and always challenging question of self-identity.

I
Identifying the Desire to Know

Whenever we are confronted with some viewpoint, attitude or expression three questions spontaneously arise: What do they mean? What good are they? Are they "realistic" or true? Usually these three questions are only implicit in the responses we make to various expressions of perspective. But in this book they will be made explicit. Specifically, the questions of meaning, value and validity will be addressed to the visions and languages associated with what is commonly called religion, and in particular to what we shall refer to as "belief."[1]

We tend to approach religious representations with the same three-pronged battery of questions that seems to permeate all of our inquiry. We ask about the multiple articulations of religion and belief that we encounter in our world in a manner more or less confusedly related to this pattern of questioning:

(1) Do they "fit my experience"? (The question of *congruity*.)
(2) Do they have any value for me and others? (The *value* question.)
(3) Do they have any grounds? (The *validity* question.)

(1) *The question of congruity.* Does a religious expression resonate with my personal and social existence in such a way as to be "meaningful" to me? Do religious stories, for example, seem to consolidate elements of my experience and smoothly integrate the multiple episodes of my life into a coherent totality? Or do they seem foreign and remote, meaningless? Do such stories arouse animating feelings and moods, or do they simply fail to move me at all? If I find that symbols and stories pertaining to religious traditions fail to evoke any sense of such inner vibrancy I will

7

probably inquire no further into them. If, however, my sensitivities are somehow awakened, I might go on to ask the other two questions.

(2) *The question of value.* Does the religious narrative or expression of belief correspond to what I consider worthwhile or conform to my sense of what is good? Do the words, rites, exhortations and basic attitudes of religious communities lead me toward or away from what I value most? Is it morally or socially wholesome to embrace and appropriate a religious vision? Is being religious being responsible?

(3) *The question of validity.* Of our three questions this is the one which, for reasons we shall see later, has the most difficulty coming to explicit expression. It asks about the reasonableness of religious points of view. It is a question that must be distinguished from the previous two. For I might find a religious statement "fitting" or "valuable" and still wonder whether it is *true*, whether it is grounded in the real. This point requires further discussion. It will be our major concern in this book to ask whether being religious or being a believer is also being reasonable.

If I were to accept a set of religious convictions I would probably not do so simply because upon reflection I thought it was reasonable to do so. I would be "converted" essentially because I felt in a pretheoretical way that there was some congruity between my experience and the language of religion. Perhaps its ritual expression, its symbols, myths and stories may have entranced me with some hidden appeal not fully accessible to theoretical reflection. I may have been caught up in the feeling that I too am part of the cosmic and historical narratives associated with some religious tradition. In short, I may simply have found a religious vision "fitting" before I was even capable of asking whether it is reasonably intelligent to align myself with it. In any case, my association with a religious community involves a being grasped by the power of *symbolic* and *narrative* utterance at a level that stirs to life long before I ask questions of validity in a deliberate way. To those of us who are theoretically oriented this is a most perplexing occurrence.

On the other hand, I may have rejected as incongruous any invitation to share in the religious dramas of others. Perhaps I was instinctively repulsed by the ceremonies of a particular sect. Maybe the stories about the Buddha, Moses, Jesus or Mohammed have meant nothing to me in terms of my feelings and desires. Thus, I may never have experienced any exigency to ask whether there are any substantial or reasonable grounds to these stories. For it is doubtful whether such a quest for the "truth" of religious accounts can seriously begin before there has been some amount of spontaneous appropriation of their content in a pretheoretical way.

When this question does arise, however, we may call it the question of the validity of religious conviction. It asks not merely how I feel about religious expressions, although it knows feeling to be an essential element in religious awareness. Nor is it concerned immediately with their function or value, even though it allows for the fact that religious life, for better or for worse, does have functional significance in the lives of individuals and society. The question of validity asks, independently of feelings and value-judgments, whether there are reasonable grounds to the claims of a religious community or whether these claims are sheer mystification. This third question arises out of a striving that seeks not only what is meaningful and useful but also what is real as distinct from illusory. It asks whether religious claims are reducible to desires, feelings, moral commitments or whether these claims have a content that transcends their aesthetic or moral appeal. Whether this question about the truth-value of religious claims leads to significant results is the central issue to be examined in this book. It is the most important element in any philosophy of religion.

The Priority of the Validity Question

What is chronologically last may be first systematically. The validity question, the question of whether being religious or being a believer is compatible with being reasonable probably arises only after one has made some implicit positive response to the questions of congruity and value. One is not always interested in asking for its grounds in reality until after he has found a religious story fitting or worthwhile. The explicit, reflective inquiry as to whether there is formal truth in religious statements usually occurs only after one has passed tacit sentient and value-judgments on them.

From a systematic point of view, however, the third question, that of validity, is prior to the others.

By this I mean that unless the language of religion or of belief in God can satisfy my craving for the real, for being, it is doubtful whether it can more than momentarily appeal to my aesthetic tastes and moral concerns.

A set of unfounded statements may have initial aesthetic, sentient or moral appeal that makes me inclined to accept them also as valid. But once they are shown to be unfounded and adventitious, they tend to lose their former aura of being "fitting" or worthwhile. Not every "bright" idea, Bernard Lonergan insists, turns out to be a true idea.[2] And once an apparently ingenious or noble idea is demonstrated to be without reasonable grounds, its brightness begins to pale and fade away. Its semblance of felt congruity and its moral appeal vanish. Scientists have sometimes had the experience of fabricating beautifully intriguing hypotheses that, taken in isolation from a rigorous attention to data, exhibit remarkable patterns appealing to aesthetic sensitivity. But when and if such hypotheses are seen to be unrelated to the data of experience, that is, when they are falsified, they immediately lose their façade of beauty and coherence also.

How many "believers" have felt the warmth of their visceral acceptance of religious expression subside as they subjected it to the critiques of modern social science and philosophy? Even though a great deal of tenderness and security may have been instilled in consciousness by a religious mentality, many people feel it is dishonest to accept it unless it can also be shown to be reasonable. And since being reasonable seems to these same people to demand total acceptance of the modern spirit of criticism embodied by the sciences, they are willing to sacrifice meaning and security for the sake of what they consider to be the best standards of truth. Unless religious visions satisfy the need to know in addition to other needs, they cannot fully appeal to those who are seeking to be reasonable and not just secure in their lives.

An illustration of this point comes from a self-styled unbeliever. His statement makes an important point:

I can sympathize with people's need for religion, but to me, their acceptance of it is wishful thinking, if it involves thinking at all. I have little sympathy for those who embrace a wa-tered-down version of religion, who interpret its texts "symbol-ically," and who partake of its rituals "culturally." If they cannot accept it intellectually, why fool around? "As if" reli-gion strikes me as an exercise in futility.[3]

Religion, this writer is saying, may seem symbolically fitting and culturally worthwhile. But if one cannot accept its claims as valid, according to solid intellectual criteria, then it is phony to defend it as fitting or meritorious. The question of validity takes priority over those of congruity and value.

Not everyone, however, recognizes this hierarchy in the struc-ture of our questions. The question of truth does not always appear uppermost in the reflections of even some of the most prominent philosophers. Alfred North Whitehead, for example, holds that ". . . in the real world it is more important that a proposition be interesting than that it be true. The importance of truth is, that it adds to interest."[4]

This point of view does seem to fit a psychological portrait of knowing. But it is inadequate, or at least misleading, as a philo-sophical statement about knowing. For the interest that proposi-tions hold for us is contingent upon our anticipation of their con-formity to reality. When we face up to the unreality of a statement or conviction, it also loses its interest. As far as religious assertions are concerned it is especially doubtful whether they would be in-teresting to the religious man did he not, from the very first aware-ness of them, anticipate their validity. In what sense such asser-tions may be judged to be valid, however, is the most troubling question facing the philosopher of religion.

"It is not self-evident," W.T. Stace wrote in 1948, ". . . that truth is the supreme value to which all else must be sacrificed. Might not the discoverer of a truth which would be fatal to man-kind be justified in suppressing it, even in teaching men a false-hood? Is truth more valuable than goodness and beauty and happi-ness?"[5]

This tendency to disengage goodness, beauty and happiness from our inborn interest in the truth will be subjected to lengthy

questioning in the following pages. Any critique of religious consciousness must seriously ponder the common impulse to suppose
that man's thirst for the real can be so casually subordinated to
aesthetic and moral concerns. There are innumerable philosophers
today who hold to a view similar to that of Stace when it comes to
reflection on religious convictions. Religion, they concede, is acceptable in terms of our pursuit of goodness, beauty and happiness. However, it cannot be accepted as a solution to our quest for
truth.

Religious man, however, if we take him at his word, envisions
his convictions to be true. Religious expressions would not inspire
goodness, nor satisfy the religious man's quest for beauty and happiness if he put in brackets the question of their truth. It is his
spontaneous commitment to their truth-value that arouses specifically religious feelings and moral or aesthetic responses. Religious
myth gives man absolute reality according to Eliade.[6] It is impossible for the religious man to accept the exhortation of the philosopher to suspend any judgments of the validity of his statements
while still adhering to their moral, social and aesthetic value. Once
the truth of a religious vision is made questionable, then its fittingness and value must also be questioned.

If the philosopher is to defend religious life in any sense, and
in an honest way, he must be able to show how it supports and
promotes the mind's quest for what is real. If there is any sense in
which religion sabotages this quest, then the only coherent stance
the philosopher can take with respect to it is to reject it as illusory.
And if religion is sheer illusion, it is difficult to understand how, in
the long run, it can be meaningful or valuable either. Our reasons
for making this statement should become clearer as we proceed.

The validity question, then, is systematically prior to questions of congruity and value, even though it might not arise as systematic until after aesthetic and moral interests have been noticed.
The question of the grounds for religious convictions or belief is
philosophically prior to that of the motives for them.

The Roots of Method

Since this book has as its central task the raising of critical
questions about religious phenomena and expressions of belief, it is

essential that we become clear as to what types of questions we are asking and how these questions are to be structured and interrelated. Although a philosophy of religion cannot provide its own starting point, and must begin with life as it is lived spontaneously, it may at least furnish its own method. So before we go any further, I am obliged to clarify the method that will be employed in the following chapters. My intention is to show that this method is not an arbitrary one, that the reader's own critical capacities correspond to this method, and that the three questions we have already ushered forth spring spontaneously and inescapably from a method that is latent and invariant in the human mind itself.

Our method involves first of all attending to the given structures, imperatives and dynamics of the human mind itself.[7] That there are such *given* spontaneous elements may be verified if the reader is willing to undertake a short experiment in self-awareness.

The experiment referred to is one that we shall continually draw upon in the course of this work. It is most elaborately construed in Lonergan's *Insight*, and I am merely utilizing and adapting a brief segment of it here.[8] I shall presume that most readers have never before been asked to undertake this specific type of self-reflection. And I shall also sympathize with those whose immediate reaction will be to wonder at the apparently innocuous results. For few people are even interested in how their minds spontaneously work unless they anticipate something momentous to be promised by such knowledge. Entering into cognitional self-analysis can be ventured with enthusiasm only if such an exercise has some goal of considerable personal interest. The goal that I think is of maximum interest to nearly everyone is that of self-acceptance; and it is ultimately toward this that the following is directed.

I extend to the reader the possibility that through this sensitization to his own knowing processes he may come into deeper possession of himself. The reward is self-knowledge and, if successful, a new degree of self-acceptance. I hold this out not as a guarantee but only as a possibility. For coming to reflective awareness of what one already spontaneously is, is a slow and even painful process. Its success ultimately rests upon the openness and courage one can achieve to face himself in depth.

Perhaps, though, I can offer the reader another incentive for embarking on this excursion into his cognitional life. One does not have to have lived very long today before he poses the (actually ancient and recurrent) question: is not everything relative? Is there any firm ground to stand on? This question is of particular urgency to those who at one time or another have felt secure, even absolutely certain, about their religious convictions. Yet through exposure to others' interpretations of human existence they now have the sensation of floating aimlessly in a dizzying whirlpool of points of view. None of these seem to be fully convincing, and all of them have at least something to say. And those who have become sensitive to the thought of Camus, Sartre and Freud or to alternative religious attitudes, to modern history and social science experience this relativity often with great loss of self-confidence. In fact at times it seems that the more open they are to new opinions, the more their powers of discrimination recede. When this happens the search for some foothold upon which to secure their world easily becomes a pathetic obsession. The quest for stability and meaning, then, involves a sacrifice of deep layers of self-awareness and the premature frustration of some of the most vital human strivings. One needs to make his way out of the flux somehow, and the easiest exit is fanaticism.

The cognitional self-awareness toward which we are working demands a firm renunciation of the temptation to escape the emptiness of relativism by way of fanatical retreat to lost certitudes. Such a reversion is symptomatic of a lack of self-awareness and the confidence that may accompany a deep knowledge of oneself as a knower. By settling down prematurely in a world of absolute certitude that one has not appropriated cognitionally as well as viscerally one may find that the reprieve from vertigo is only ephemeral. But by awakening to himself as a knower he finds a center of stillness within the vortex of possible world perspectives. An appreciative understanding of one's cognitional acts and the dynamic drive underlying these can provide each individual with a standpoint from which he may enter into the veritable swamp of cultural, intellectual and religious alternatives without fear of being engulfed by relativism or crippled by the obsession with certitude.

The reflective appropriation of the dynamics of the human

mind involves, as we shall try to show, the simultaneous disclosure of that from which our sense of the relativity of things flows. It is the striving current of our own minds that pushes us away from one certitude in search of others. A sympathetic and courageous participation in the mind's spontaneous thrusting forward through its irrepressible questions does not rescue us from the flux. But it may allow us to realize that there would be no sense of relativity without the dynamic center in the self that continually strives for more knowledge and to which our forays of experience always return for insight and assent.

Now that from which our sense of relativity derives cannot be simply one element among others in our experience. It is the very source of the horizon over against which relativity shows up as such. Thus our journey into self-awareness can lead us out of relativism at the same time that it repudiates the obsessive demand for certitude. There is a sense in which the philosophic excursion we are about to enter upon shares with the religious wisdom of the East the quest for a point of stillness at the center of the vortex. But we shall find that this center is also one that continually directs us outward into the flux without making us drift aimlessly in it.

Method and Cognitional Self-Awareness[9]

The method followed in this book is one that fits the demands of any fully functioning human mind. It is not, therefore, an imposition upon the reader of questions contrived by the author. It is a method that can be formulated only simultaneously with the discernment of the spontaneous self-structuring of our questioning. Method, according to Lonergan, may be understood as a set of directives guiding a process toward a result.[10] But if such a set of directives is to avoid arbitrariness it must conform at the very minimum to the mind's own demands and structures. That there are such demands and structures (involving differentiated, but complementary components) may be authenticated if the reader will reflect momentarily on his own thinking and knowing process which up until this point has been indeliberate and unreflected. Such reflection, guided by our suggestions, will provide the foundation for any method involving the use of the human mind. It will, therefore, expose the directives calling forth the types of questions that we shall address to man's religious life. And as a result it will allow the reader to participate more fully in our inquiries into religion and belief.

For purposes of emphasis, if the reader will allow, I shall make a brief transition to second-person discourse.

If you have followed me up to this point you will note that your mind has been working instinctively and involuntarily. You have not been reflecting upon or interfering with its natural, fluid maneuverings. But now look back, take note of, try to grasp and understand the sequential pattern of your spontaneous thinking, questioning, reflecting and judging. You will find that your acts of thinking and knowing have followed this order of arrangement:

(1) First you have attended to and experienced the words of this book through the medium of your senses. You have been, in some way, perceptive and open to the data before you. This first level of cognition we shall call simply *experience*.

(2) Then your mind spontaneously (without any deliberate, methodical coercion) brought forth the question as to what these words, sentences and paragraphs are all about. What intelligibility, if any, is there to be grasped on these pages? The struggle for insight emerged. You may find yourself still scrambling to understand what is being said here. Perhaps no insight has yet occurred. But my point is that your questioning has moved you from sheer experience of the data (the words of this book) to an attempt to understand them. And this, I repeat, has happened spontaneously. You did not force the question, "What is this all about?" to arise. It came forth without any inhibition or compulsion. The second level in the sequence of cognitional acts, intended by the questions for intelligence, is called *understanding*. It takes shape in what we call insights. And these insights are elaborated in concepts, propositions, formulations, hypotheses, theories, etc.

(3) By this time you may be wondering whether what I have just stated is correct. Or you may be asking whether your own understanding of what I have said is accurate. In either case you have spontaneously asked a type of question which is subtly different from that which gave rise to the second level. You have asked a

reflective, or critical, question: "Is my understanding *correct* understanding?" After you have achieved an initial insight and formulated it in a concept you still feel the need to ask whether your initial insight is faithful to the data of your experience. For example, is your understanding of what I have written faithful to the meaning I have intended? When and if you answer this question your answer will be expressed through a third cognitional act, that of *judgment*. Judging is not the same thing as understanding, even though many philosophers have not adverted to the difference. For after you have performed an act of understanding the data of your experience, you still have a natural exigency to ask whether your understanding is faithful to the data of experience. As we shall see, this need to ask critically reflective questions about our insights is not always allowed to surface. But there is some light in all of us which compels us to recognize a difference between thinking and knowing. To make the transition from sheer thought to knowledge we must somehow grasp through a *reflective* insight the correctness or inaccuracy of our first, or direct insight. And it is in the act of judgment that we express this reflective grasp of the fulfillment of those conditions required for the act of assent or negation. It is in judgment that our thinking is accepted as knowledge of the real and not mere speculation.

Experience gives us only data, not understanding or facts. Understanding gives us insight, not necessarily reality or factual knowledge. It is our acts of affirmation or negation in judging, and not mere experience or understanding, that express our being in touch with reality. Facts are arrived at only through judgment and not from mere looking or hypothesizing. When we say that "such and such is the case" a whole world of meaning is implied in that "is" which we seldom reflect upon but which will have a significant bearing on the questions to be discussed in this book.

(4) Intimately associated with human knowing is human acting. Many of our actions flow from what we call decisions. But decisions are not arbitrary. Those actions of ours that are arbitrary are rooted in impulse and not decision. What keeps decisions from being arbitrary is that they are somehow related to the first three levels of consciousness: experience, understanding and judgment. This relationship is quite complex and we need not dwell on it

here. We shall simply take note of a fourth act, that of *decision*, which is intimately related to the three previous levels of cognitional structure. It is the act that mediates between human knowing and human doing.

It will be objected that my articulation of this structure is culturally conditioned and therefore open to revision. Accordingly it may not seem to escape the relativity associated with any other account. It provides no exit from the flux.

I would readily concede that my language and concerns are "situated," that they possess no absoluteness or universality insofar as they emerge from a particular time in history and from within the culture of the West. At the same time, however, it is difficult to conceive how the above scheme could ever be revised without its being employed by the agent of the revision. I think we have here a "fixed base" immune to relativization. For any attempt to revise or relativize it would itself involve experience, understanding, judgment and decision.[11] Appropriation of this base may be one way of gaining a foothold in a fluid and restless world.

Imperatives Rooted in Cognitional Structure

Without your ever having reflected on it before, you may now advert to the fact that your spontaneous, yet unavoidable, adherence to the above sequence of cognitional acts is the result of an unreflective awareness of imperatives that are given with your consciousness itself. I would invite you now to bring these imperatives forward in your reflection since these will be essential operative tools for our critical approach to religious phenomena. These imperatives with their consequent cognitional acts are as follows:[12]

(1) Be attentive! (Be open!)→ experience
                                   ↓ ↑
(2) Be intelligent!   → under-
                             standing ↓ ↑
(3) Be reflective! (Be critical!)→ judgment
                                   ↓ ↑
(4) Be responsible!   → decision

(Note also the arrows pointing upward. These are intended to portray the interpenetration of the four levels of consciousness. The imperative "be responsible," for example, urges one to be ever more attentive, intelligent and reflective. It is not simply the last in a series of acts. The acts of cognition and decision constitute a functional and structural complementarity.[13] And the imperatives all flow, as we shall see, from a single source.)

These imperatives have obliged you to raise the questions you find yourself asking all the time, questions for intelligence, reflection and decision. Perhaps you have never reflected on your knowing activity in this way before. It may never have occurred to you that your spontaneous inquiry and learning was a response to these hidden but persistent imperatives. And even now you may be asking, "so what?" (This question of course is further evidence of your spontaneous urge to seek intelligibility in response to the second precept: be intelligent!) You cannot escape from these "transcendental imperatives." For even when you question whether you can, you are doing so in obedience to them (being attentive, intelligent and critical). But rather than seeing yourself as hemmed in by these inescapable directives, you may eventually be able to accept them as the foundation of what is called human freedom. Their intention is always to open consciousness up to newer and richer experience, to enlarge our world and expand our possibilities for action. A reflective appropriation and humble acceptance of these imperatives seems to me to be the primary goal of philosophy. And when the philosopher approaches the data of religious life his most direct concern is how religion relates to the world-enlargement toward which the imperatives of his mind instinctively move. Does religious life promote or frustrate the goals of these innate and irremovable precepts?

The above scheme would perhaps be inconsequential, and our disclosure of its native invariance in man's consciousness would be without import were it not for the obvious and perplexing fact that we humans are continually violating its norms. We are not always sufficiently attentive, intelligent and critical, let alone responsible. The evasion of understanding, the "flight from insight," is a pervasive temptation. Thus our bringing the above structure into reflection is intended to make us more aware of what is involved both in the quest for the real and the flight from it. Above all, at this point in our inquiry, it is intended to establish part of the framework necessary for a critique of religious awareness.

When the topic under reflective scrutiny is man's religious life, our questions cannot be other than those that our minds naturally produce. Our questions about religion and belief must follow the imperatives given with consciousness. And, however it structures itself in its details, an inquiry into the phenomenon of religious existence must at the very least allow scope for the full range of questions flowing out of the mind's innate requirements. I am not at all convinced that such a scope has been allowed for in much so-called philosophy of religion.

The three questions that we asked earlier about the data of religious expression arise out of the imperatives embedded irremovably in our conscious striving. In a preliminary way the precept "be attentive" urges us to be open to the religious experience in as unbiased a manner as possible. Phenomenological approaches to religion have been especially responsive to this imperative, but they have not always been sufficiently alert to the others. Then the imperative "be intelligent" calls for continued insight into the data of the various scientific and phenomenological approaches to religion. It calls for theories of religion's origins, for example. It seeks to formulate the place of religion in human consciousness. It is out of this demand that the question arises of the congruity of religious attitudes in terms of human experience. Next, the critical exigency calls forth the question of the validity of religious statements. The philosopher expresses a need to know whether his or others' religious ideas are mere thinking or whether they somehow manifest real knowledge. This leads him to ask whether being religious is consistent with being reasonable. And, finally, the philosopher also feels the obligation to be responsible. It is out of his groping attempts to heed this imperative that he asks about the value of religious acts. In order to assist him in this task he calls upon the social scientist and others who are interested in the relationship of religion to the well-being of man.

Thus there is more to a philosophy of religion than mere attentiveness to it as a phenomenon. Recent phenomenological studies of religion are sometimes made to pass as philosophies of religion simply because they are allegedly more open and attentive to the data of religious awareness than traditional studies have been. While the attentiveness stressed by phenomenology in most of its forms is laudable (and is homogeneous with the birth of philosophical wisdom in the openness of wonder), it must not attempt to edge out theories and critiques of religion. Attentiveness to religion as a phenomenon is not enough to constitute a philosophy of religion for it does not adequately satisfy the imperatives to be intelligent, critical and responsible. Philosophy cannot disengage its concerns from these.

There is a widespread conviction that religious knowledge occupies so privileged an area in consciousness that critical questions may not be addressed to it. There are those who hold that a philosophy of religion has nothing to offer the religious man, that it is just another attempt to escape the personal commitment necessary for a religious way of life. The philosopher appears so detached from the feelings, concerns and ideas of religious man that the philosopher is not able to enter into any meaningful reflection on religion. If religion is to be criticized it must be done from within a milieu generated by faith and not by reflection.

This objection is premised on the assumption that philosophical interests cannot coincide with religious ones. It takes note of the fact that many philosophers of religion have often eviscerated the specifically religious act and impaled it on a theoretical structure of understanding where its content is altogether lost sight of. And it notes that often philosophers have even attempted to substitute their own abstract notions of the absolute for religious ones.

We have already renounced this approach, and we have insisted that philosophical reflection must recognize that the notions of God or the sacred are born in religious acts, not theoretical ones. The whole problem of the God of the philosophers versus the God of religion is a false one.[14] And as Duméry says:

> . . . it is incomprehensible that a philosopher would study the idea of the Absolute without referring to spiritual experience, that is to the process of conversion that initiates . . . the religious attitude in general.[15]

Although philosophy has often blundered especially in its failure to attend fully to the religious act, it has not necessarily lost its right or forfeited its obligation to criticize religion. To do so would be to abandon its role in human life altogether. The basic duty of the philosopher is that of alerting us to and fostering the interests of the imperatives that our brief reflections on the knowing process have brought forth. This means that the philosopher has the right and the obligation to ask whether and how the various affirmations of the sacred relate to the mind's imperatives. It is not a violation of the possible integrity of the religious act to ask whether and in what way being religious might help man accept these precepts. When the philosoper asks whether being religious is being reasonable, this is a legitimate question provided that its meaning is as follows: Is being religious consistent with being open, insightful, critical and responsible? In those cases where it is not, religious man needs the iconoclasm of the philosopher. And, as we shall see, there are numerous instances where religious attitudes have been utilized as ways of hiding from the mind's imperatives. As this book develops, the reader will note that we vigorously reject any attempt to substitute the theoretical for the religious. But this does not imply that our theoretical reflections can have no positive influence on the way in which religion serves the mind's imperatives, and ultimately, therefore, on its role in the process of self-acceptance.

Identifying the Desire to Know[16]

We have now arrived at the point where we may give a name to that dynamic stirring which, from deep within, unceasingly prods consciousness with its imperatives. Call it simply the *desire to know*. The desire to know is the time-honored phrase we shall use to refer to the elusive, intangible source of the precepts and questions that lead us toward knowledge and responsible decision. We shall refer to it alternatively as the *pure* desire to know in order to distinguish it from other desires. From antiquity philosophers have also called it wonder. But by using the equally ancient term "desire," we are able to accentuate the dynamic, restless and irrepressible character of what might well be our basic drive.

Hopefully by now you have enlivened your awareness of the

already active desire to know expressed through the imperatives that you may easily identify in your consciousness. In this desire you have at least one point of reference in terms of which you may attempt to locate how religious intuition "fits" into man's consciousness. What relationship do religious feelings, knowledge, images and stories have to that dynamic, irrepressible core of consciousness that we are referring to as the desire to know?

I have not yet identified what I have been alluding to as religious awareness. It is only with fear and trembling that anyone can venture to do so. What I am attempting in this first chapter and in much of the second is preliminary to such identification. Any notion or description of religion must be explicated in terms of what is identified as human consciousness in the broadest sense. Thus, in bringing attention to the desire to know out of which the reader's own knowledge of the world unfolds, we are trying to disclose a firm foundation, perceptible to anyone adverting to his own cognitional performance, in terms of which we can talk about and reflect upon "religious" thought. We might have approached man's religious life from the point of view of how it relates to other desires that are also immediately discernible. The desire for pleasure, the will to meaning, or the impulse to control, for example, are usefully employed as alternative points of departure for understanding religious data. And in the following chapters we shall discuss those theories of religion that attempt to root the sense of the sacred in some such desire. However, I think that a more thoroughgoing endeavor to get to the roots of religious longing involves at some point a study of the question of how it relates to the desire to know.

I know of few studies of religion that give an extended treatment of this relationship.[17] The reasons for this are complex. Often, however, there is a hidden bias that religion has little to do with reasonableness. The classic division of human faculties into intellect, will and affect is partly responsible for this theoretical isolation of religion from rational striving. And it is understandable, given this faculty psychology, that conflicts have been aroused between religion and philosophy, faith and knowledge, spirituality and rationality. But by rooting consciousness in a *desire* to know we can transcend the separation of the faculties while still allowing for their distinctions. The imperatives of the mind, for example, lead to distinct acts, but they are all rooted in a single source. The desire to know is itself a striving, and therefore inseparable from affect and volition. And the desire to know is ultimately a desire for the good. According to Aristotle,

> Every art and every inquiry, and similarly every action and pursuit seems to aim at some good. Consequently the Good has rightly been said to be that at which all things aim.[18]

If, then, our various cognitional and volitional acts are grounded in the unity of striving for what is good, then what turns us toward the good converts us also toward the true, toward the reasonable. It is in this light that we must ask about the reasonableness of religion.

Many philosophers and also some theologians would instinctively shy away from any enterprise that even hints at a positive relationship between religion and rational desire. As I have already indicated, however, unless there is an intimacy between religion and the desire to know, there is no conceivable way in which religious persons and communities can escape the charge of wishful thinking, of flight from reality.

II
Religion and the Elements of Consciousness

There is a distinct advantage to beginning a critical investigation of religious consciousness from the point of view of the desire to know. It consists in the fact that the most characteristic aspect of this desire, one which radically differentiates it from other strivings, is its natural intention of the real. Unlike other desires with which we are familiar, the desire to know can never remain satisfied with illusion. Its very essence is to cut through what other passions would *like* to be real. Its restlessness continually prods us to distinguish insights, ideas and thinking from genuine knowing. Thus advertance to it is necessary when we ask about the "truth" of religious knowledge.

Especially through its injunction to "be critical," the desire to know gives evidence of its inherent detachment. By detachment I mean that aspect of the desire to know which lifts it out of the privacy of self-interest deriving from adherence to alien and fugitive inclinations. In and of itself the pure desire to know is willing to disengage itself from what would satisfy only other desires. It pursues the truth even when it hurts. In this sense the desire to know may also be called disinterested. So when we use the expression "desire to know," the adjectives "pure," "detached," and "disinterested," are understood.[1]

To say that the desire to know is detached and disinterested could easily lead to a misunderstanding. We do not mean to imply that this desire is passionless or lifeless. On the contrary, it is most lively, and we shall present numerous examples of prominent thinkers whose very vitality and spirit derives from their attachment to this drive. Indeed the desire to know is the most fervent orientation in many people's lives. If the desire to know is detached, it is only because it is also involved, passionately interested in the "real" and contemptuous of fanciful, illusory thinking. It can and does solicit the dynamics and services of biological and psychic sources of excitement to bear it toward its goal. It is not, therefore, separable from affect and passion. Thus Plato names it Eros.

Essentially the desire to know is detached from those impulses that urge us to take refuge in bias and illusion. Existentially, however, that is to say in the concrete, the desire to know must continually wrestle with opposing tendencies. While it is essentially pure and detached, in actual fact it is always countered by ignorance and error. At times the organic, psychic and interpersonal drift of human awareness will impede and even contradict its natural intentionality. Every person has to struggle to disentangle the innate leanings of this desire from more primitive orientations. And it is only when one has become personally and painfully convinced that "the truth shall set you free," that he courageously tries to conform to the sometimes severe imperatives of his consciousness. The desire to know is undoubtedly a most difficult drive to accept and adjust to. As Kierkegaard puts it:

> . . . it is far from being the case that men in general regard relationship to the truth, as the highest good, and it is far from being the case that they, Socratically, regard being under a delusion as the greatest misfortune.[2]

Nonetheless, the ineradicable intention of the desire to know is "reality." In fact, the word "reality" makes sense only if it is understood as the objective of the desire to know. (If the reader finds himself questioning whether this is so, it is because his own desire to know seeks what is "really" the case). Our basic drive can never be content with what is suspected to be illusory. Many other desires may attempt to interfere with it and may even nearly succeed in burying it. But in and of itself its intended goal is reality. There is even a sense in which it is a desire for all reality, for the plenitude of being. Essentially, therefore, the desire to know is unrestricted in its objective. Nothing lies beyond its virtual scope.[3]

Is religious life an ally of or an obstacle to the free flow of this desire? How is it possible to determine which religious manifestations would arise out of this desire and which would spring from some opposing or contrasting passion? Is religion an escape from reality? Is it to be explained exhaustively in terms of the Freudian pleasure principle, or of a will to power or the need to have meaning? By bringing religious inclinations into confrontation with what must be the most intractable desire surging up within us, the pure desire to know, we are each in a position to give a critique of religion from a deeply personal perspective. And we are also able to gain some understanding of how religion originates in terms of conscious activity. Any discussion of these points, however, involves further determination of what we mean by "religion" and by "consciousness."

Religion

In the past century theories of religion have multiplied. And there is no universal consensus on how best to understand a phenomenon with so broad a range of manifestations. Typically religion is understood in the Western world as involving "belief in God." But there are many places on this earth where "religious" attitudes have prevailed for centuries without any reference to a transcendent, personal power like that represented by Western theism. The incredible diversity of religious forms makes the quest for a common essence a most frustrating one.

Still many attempts have been made to formulate the *essence* of religion. It is impossible here to enter into the complex history of these scholarly endeavors. The very word "religion" has a history that tells of repeated and awkward attempts to objectify a phenomenon which has concrete existence only in the transitory personalities of participants in the various traditions. (And these traditions also have an elusive mode of existence at the intersection between real persons and the texts, monuments or other inherited sediments of religious life.[4]) Locating "religion" in man's life is itself a delicate task.

Even though we cannot summarize the tortuous history of the notion of religion, we may briefly sketch three general classes of attempts to understand the fundamental element in religious awareness. These three groups represent the movement from a specifically Western theistic orientation through a taking into account of other "religions" of the world's history, to an attempt to embrace under the category of religion also those types of commitment that many would judge to be purely secular.[5]

(1) A first meaning given to the word "religion" is simply faith in God. This of couse is the usage especially familiar to those in the tradition of biblical "religion." Philosophically and theologically formulated, this religion is often called theism. But because of the pejorative connotations of this term in many modern circles, we shall prefer the term "belief" to designate the act of affirmation of a transcendent, personal God as in Judaism and Christianity. We shall be especially interested in the relationship of this belief to the desire to know. And the final chapters of this book will explicitly reflect upon the meaning, validity and value of this specific type of religious affirmation.

(2) A broader meaning of the term "religion" is suggested especially by the work of Mircea Eliade, Rudolf Otto, Gerardus Van der Leeuw and their followers. It takes into account experience of the "sacred" in the non-biblical world as well as the religious experience of the West. Briefly stated religion is the act or attitude of constituting the *sacred* as a realm distinct but not separate from the profane. Religious ritual and discourse, religious "experience" in general is characterized by a sense of the sacred, or of the "holy" (Rudolf Otto)[6] dialectically related to the profane (Eliade).[7] Anything profane can mediate or symbolize the awesome and fascinating presence of the sacred, superhuman but not necessarily "personal" power. The holy confronts man through profane objects and persons as a *"mysterium tremendum et fascinans."* And the normatively religious response, according to this view, is one of acknowledgment of creatureliness or a sense of dependency upon the sacred.[8] This description of religion is capable of embracing a biblical notion of God the Creator equally as well as a Melanesian experience of *mana*.

(3) A still more comprehensive notion of religion is given in the writings of Paul Tillich.[9] This notion also has received wide acceptance even though it encounters resistance especially among

some of the advocates of the first and second approaches. Religion in this view is the state of being ultimately concerned. Ultimate concern, however, is not limited to explicit commitment to an intangible sacred force or to God. One can make any object into an ultimate without envisioning it as dialectically symbolic of some sacred, transempirical source of power. The attitude of ultimate concern can be directed toward any imaginable phenomenon including the purely secular. Thus pursuit of money, sex, success, etc., can be called "religious" if it expresses ultimate concern. Nationalism, secularism, Communism, Nazism, humanism, etc., as well as theism may all be included under the category of religion.

All men, in this third view, are "religious" since they tend to make something into an unconditional and unquestioned source of meaning for their lives. It is simply the quest for meaning that makes man naturally religious. But this still raises the question whether meaning can be found in a decisive way apart from commitment to the "sacred" or to "God." In other words, can religion in the third sense be ultimately intelligible unless it implies religion at least in the second sense if not also in the first?

In this book we shall be especially concerned with those expressions of ultimate concern and acknowledgment of the sacred that take the form of belief in the God of biblical religion and its derivatives. In the cultural context within which most of us have been raised, religion usually has something to do with "belief in God." I see no decisive reason for objection to this usage provided that we also remain aware of the other meanings given to the term "religion." And while the word "God" itself evokes a variety of images, it is, nevertheless, the most important element in the religious environment with which most of us are familiar. Consequently, the focus of our critique will be on this particular type of witness to the sacred.

Our objective, as I have said, will be to determine the relationship between religion and the imperatives of the mind. This, I think, is the main function of a philosophy of religion. In biblical religion there are two fundamental images associated with the name of God that will be of special significance in this inquiry. These are the images of God as Creator and Redeemer. In the consciousness of the believer the first image normatively evokes the response of grateful acceptance of his creatureliness. And the second image intends to draw forth the feeling and conviction by the believer that he is accepted "in spite of being unacceptable" (Tillich).[10] We shall ask whether a consciousness shaped by these responses and resonant with the biblical images is going to be more inclined or less inclined to give way to the desire to know than is a consciousness which recoils from these responses. And since the natural objective of the desire to know is "reality," we shall be able in this way to ascertain whether such religiously symbolic discourse is "realistic" or illusory, i.e., whether it fosters or frustrates the desire to know.

A philosophy of religion may address only one set of data at a time. It must be regional and specific. Because of our growing awareness of the diversity of the elements included under the label "religious," the most we can do is ask about the congruity, value and validity of particular images and stories associated with the individual traditions. It would be pretentious and even absurd for a philosopher to make a case for or against religion in general, since it would be impossible for us to tell what he was talking about.

I have chosen for examination the biblical affirmation of God as Creator and Redeemer. But even these images hold significations that have evolved and dramatically shifted in their over three-thousand year history. Ideally we would have to take these developments into account. However, in spite of their various meanings in the traditions flowing from the Old and New Testaments, in Judaism, in Catholic and Protestant history, it is safe to generalize on the responses they have invited from believers at all times. We shall simply refer to these responses as (1) a grateful appreciation of the sense of creatureliness and (2) acceptance of "redemption" from some threat, usually involving the sense of guilt. And we shall ask throughout the following chapters what these responses might have to do with the dynamic structure of consciousness in its pursuit of the real.

Since these two responses (which may eventually be reduced to one) are also in some sense characteristic of much if not all religious witnessing to the "sacred," our critique should be applicable, to a degree, to a great deal of religious data. I think it is important to keep our reflections anchored firmly to the particularity of religious response. For this reason I am particularly interested in what I have called "belief." And as I use the adjective "religious" subsequently, I am using it especially with reference to those responses associated with the biblical imagery. Yet I think what conclusions we draw with respect to the relationship of these symbols to the desire to know, may also be applicable *mutatis mutandis* to other forms of religious symbolism than those of biblical religion.

Human Desires

We are going to ask how religious belief correlates with the dynamics and structures of human consciousness. In this section we shall try to expand our understanding of consciousness by considering the complex spectrum of human desires. And, in the following section, we shall describe some of the fields of meaning through which our consciousness of the world is amplified. Our objective in these brief sketches is to set the stage for asking how religious awareness "fits" into our conscious life and whether it is beneficial, harmful or indifferent to our most vital strivings.

In addition to the pure desire to know that we find already active, always pushing forward with its imperatives and questions, there are also other spontaneous desires. Students of religion have inquired at times whether perhaps belief originates exclusively out of one or another of these. In the following chapters we shall examine several positions which maintain that belief stems exclusively from such dynamic drives as the will to meaning, or the need for pleasure or from some other nonrational form of libido. We shall note the utter complexity of human spontaneities and the corresponding difficulty of determining how religious belief is to be understood and evaluated in terms of their ambivalent, often mutually contradictory intentions. But we shall be essentially interested in whether there is some intimate connection between belief and the desire to know. If there is none, it would be difficult to find any validity in the claims of the believer. And, as I have tried to show, unless we can accept their validity it is difficult consistently to acclaim their symbolic fittingness or cultural and psychic value. The inescapable imperative to be critical, which is the spearhead of the detached desire to know, forbids any such contrived harmonization. If belief is not reasonable (i.e., consistent with the third precept) then neither is it responsible.

In a preliminary way we may give simple designations to the several distinguishable but also interpenetrating desires that we shall use as part of the base for inquiry:

(1) The desire to know
(2) The desire for meaning (also to be called, following William James, the "will to believe")
(3) The desire for pleasure (following Freud's usage)
(4) The will to power
(5) Other psychic and social desires

Although there is an obvious underlying unity in any person's strivings, there is also the possibility of disharmony and disproportion among the manifold desires. Thus it is meaningful to make distinctions among them. Since these distinctions will be brought out in the chapters that follow there is no need to dwell on them here. We need only note briefly that philosophers often make such distinctions among our desires.

Plato, for example, differentiates between *epithumia* (sensible desire) and *eros* (rational desire).[11] And Aristotle follows in discriminating between the element of pleasure and the element of happiness in our activity. The striving for pleasure shows up as distinct from a striving for happiness, according to Aristotle, because pleasure is perfected in finite acts of enjoyment whereas the quest for happiness is a continuing, ongoing process realized only in what the philosopher calls contemplation.[12] And, commenting on this, Paul Ricoeur reflects:

> If one does not take into consideration the primordial disproportion of vital desire and intellectual love (or of spiritual joy), one entirely misses the specific nature of human affectivity. Man's humanity is not reached by adding one more stratum to the basic substratum of tendencies (and affective states) which are assumed to be common to animal and man. Man's humanity is that discrepancy in levels, that initial polarity, that divergence of affective tension between the extremities of which is placed the "heart."[13]

Ricoeur is here alluding to one of the characteristics of finitude that makes fallibility possible. The ineradicable disproportion between rational desire (the desire to know) and the drive for pleasure is not itself "evil," but it is a condition that makes the positing of evil a possibility.

> Human action aims both at a self-sufficient totality which would give, which would be beatitude, the enjoyment of happiness, and a finite realization in discrete acts, in "results" sanctioned by a consciousness of success or pleasure. The repose in pleasure threatens to bring the dynamism of activity to a standstill and screen the horizon of happiness.[14]

Numerous other philosophers and, especially today, psychologists have highlighted the potentially conflictual nature of our desiring. The role that religious imagination often plays in human conflicts, therefore, requires that we consult especially those who envision religion in terms of one desire or another. It is not merely the task of the social scientist but also of the philosopher of religion to formulate the relationship between religion and human desire. For if we follow a strong tradition running through Plato, Aristotle, medieval and modern thought, philosophy itself is a product of the desire to know. And the philosopher must dutifully ask whether religion is a help or a hindrance to the happiness which this desire holds out to those who choose to follow it wherever it leads.

In this sense a philosophy of religion is committed to asking whether religion makes for *happiness* as the state promised by fidelity to the imperatives of the mind. Happiness is not a condition which, like pleasure, can be achieved in a discrete act. But there are certain experiences that point in the direction of happiness: "The events which bespeak happiness are those which remove obstacles and uncover a vast landscape of existence."[15] Is religious conversion ever such an event? Is it possible for reason to ask and decide which religious phenomena point toward genuine happiness or are signs thereof? Ricoeur's position on this matter is clear, and it may serve as the justification for a philosophy of religion:

. . . I could not make out these signs or interpret them as "transcending anticipations" of happiness if reason, in me, were not the demand for totality. Reason demands totality, but the instinct for happiness, insofar as it is a feeling which anticipates its realization more than it provides it, assures me that I am *directed toward* the very thing that reason *demands*. Reason opens up the dimension of totality, but the consciousness of direction, experienced in the feeling of happiness, assures me that this reason is not alien to me, that it coincides with my destiny, that it is interior to it and, as it were, coeval with it.[16]

The measure of fidelity to the desire to know, Ricoeur seems to say, is the feeling of happiness. And happiness, we shall stress, is intimately related to self-acceptance. Our inquiry into the genuineness of religious life must come back again and again to the question of its role in motivating the condition of self-acceptance necessary for a full liberation of the desire to know.

Intentional Fields

Human consciousness is opaque not only because of the interlacing of desires sometimes possessing disparate interests. It also unfolds in several distinguishable patterns of experience within which "reality" (or the "world") reveals itself in a variety of ways. The desire to know fans out, as it were, and moves down diverse cognitional and intentional channels corresponding to the complexity of the knower, the others, and the world. The desire to know intends reality. We have already verified this through our cognitional reflection in the previous chapter. (Any attempt to deny that one's desire to know intends reality is self-contradictory.) But "reality" has many different textures, and the ways by which to apprehend its nuances are manifold.

At the enormous risk of abstraction that any theoretical interpretation runs, we shall speak throughout this work of five "intentional fields." These are simply ways of reaching out for and allowing the world to come into consciousness in ways corresponding to its and the subject's depth and richness. In some

aspects this five-fold scheme draws from recent well-known phenomenological studies of cognition, but in other ways it diverges
from them.[17] The intentional fields that we shall examine are as
follows:

(1) The sentient
(2) The interpersonal
(3) The narrative
(4) The aesthetic
(5) The theoretic

Our purpose in differentiating among these patterns of experience
is that of eventually locating religious awareness in terms of the
broad scope of human consciousness in its interaction with the
world. We wish to ascertain just how, if at all, religious thinking
and belief are in the service of the desire to know, however this
desire proliferates. The richness and diversity of the patterns in
which the world comes to light originate apparently in the first
precept, "be open." Our cognition of the world, we shall see, is not
confined to the narrow perspective of theory, but rather expands
also along a spectrum of interrelated pretheoretical fields of meaning. Being attentive and open entails more than being "objective."

(1) *The sentient field.* Before we understand and know things
in a theoretical way (as does the philosopher or scientist) we live in
a world which is laid open to us by our feelings and moods. By
these I do not mean merely states reducible to psychic commotion.
I am referring to such responses to experience as anxiety, loving,
levity, hopefulness, joyfulness, feeling lonely, melancholy, etc.
These unsolicited moods are not "merely psychological." They
also have a revelatory function. Without feeling (*Gefühl, sentir*)
knowledge of our world would be impossible. We tend to dismiss
feelings as "subjective," but they must also be seen as vehicles of
the desire to know (even though they are also capable of being
exploited by other desires). We would not come into contact with
the objective or intersubjective world without a preliminary intention of this world through sentient consciousness.

Through the sympathy of feeling, the world becomes *our* reality. What is most "real" to each of us is what has been overlaid
with our own feeling. Even when much of our cognition is theoretical, we still live and think from within a world constituted by our

spontaneous prereflective stances. And if we lose touch with these sentient spontaneities by way of overemphasizing the theoretical attitude, we are headed for intellectual sterility and, perhaps, psychic disaster.

There have been theories of religion that attempt to locate religious experience entirely in the realm of feeling. Such theories do not generally make religion into something subjective in the sense of arbitrary. For they reçognize that feeling is cognitional and revelatory at the same time that it is deeply personal. F. D. Schleiermacher,[18] the best-known proponent of this view, has been often unjustly accused of subjectivism. What he was attempting, however, was to steer clear of the prevalent Enlightenment notions that religion is a mere correlate of ethics or something which could be replaced by theoretical reason. His discussion of religion in terms of feeling is still misunderstood because of our distance from the historical context of his apologetics and because of our bias that feeling is "merely subjective." Recent phenomenological restoration of the cognitional value of feeling forces us to take a more serious look at Schleiermacher today. Even though the confinement of religion in the arena of *Gefühl* appears too restrictive, there is perhaps much to be learned from a return by theories of religion to the sentient mode.

(2) *The interpersonal field:* The "world" for each one of us is inhabited by "others." Our life and thought is inextricably intertwined with other subjects. And intersubjective living with these others is an inherent aspect of our own self-understanding. As Martin Heidegger says, human existence is essentially *Mitsein*, a being-with-others.[19] Others are not just accidental elements alongside of the "world." They are constitutive of it.

The world opened up or intended by interpersonal consciousness is a world of moral concerns. Interpersonal "reality" is not apprehended as something "out there" from which I am detached, but rather as something in which I am already involved through the attitude of concern. This is an aspect of the world that is incapable of being known through the type of detachment which we usually associate with "objectivity."

Various thinkers have attempted to situate religion within this intersubjective pattern of world-involvement. Religion is then often understood as merely the expression of moral commitment. It is an essentially ethical phenomenon. The codes and commandments, the exhortation to brotherly love, and the generally ethical orientation of Semitic religions have readily given themselves over to this interpretation.

Increasingly, however, largely as a result of phenomenological studies, the view that religion is reducible to moral concern has been discredited. Even biblical religion with its "ethical monotheism" is concerned primarily with consciousness of the "sacred." And this consciousness erupts in the sentient, narrative, and aesthetic as well as in the interpersonal pattern of experience. Religion is too elusive to be confined to moral consciousness.

(3) *The narrative field:* "Reality" is not experienced apart from our moods and concerns. But these are given their specific coloring primarily by the personal and social stories in which we find our lives enfolded. The amorphous feelings with which we reach out to embrace some totality are given specific shape and direction by what I shall call narrative consciousness. It is especially from the "narrative quality of experience"[20] that we acquire our reality sense. And it is in story form that the feeling of the sacred is eventually symbolized.

Human consciousness seems to have something like a narrative *a priori* that compels us communally to experience events, places and persons in the context of some story or other.[21] Our moods and interpersonal relationships (the first two patterns) are so intimately linked to the narrative pattern of experience that if the latter is dramatically altered, the former tend to change also. The story by which we live is the integrative element determining the specific tone not only of sentient and interpersonal, but also of aesthetic and (in a sense) even theoretical awareness. So central are stories to human existence that without them life is experienced as empty and meaningless.

Because of its nuclear position in human awareness as disclosing the "world" to us, the narrative pattern of experience is the one in which we find man's religious thought and language most characteristically resident. The story, with its attendant ritual, is the most typical form of religious expression because it is through the narrative mode that men have always communicated and exchanged what is of utmost significance and concern to themselves.

The protean feeling of the sacred is molded especially in mythic and historic modes of discourse. In these narrative forms it is given specific sociocultural configuration. Some feeling of the sacred seems to have been a universal, transcultural experience at one time. Although the mythic forms in which this experience was recounted varied considerably from place to place, some feeling of the absolute, the holy, the sacred remained a constant. And the narrative mode continued to couch the experience of the holy when historic consciousness emerged in Hebrew religion.

The "stories of God" that have come down to us from Hebrew and later Jewish and Christian tradition will be of particular concern to us. The images of God as Creator and Redeemer that we have isolated are embedded in narratives of a mythic-historic nature. Granted that these stories somehow satisfy the believer's desire for meaning, can they ever satisfy the desire to know? Granted that such stories can give us a "reality sense," can they give us reality? Precisely how are such stories related to the imperatives of the mind?

(4) *The aesthetic pattern:* Our sense of wonder also takes us along the path determined by what is beautiful. The world is given to us by our language, symbols, concerns, stories and traditions, but also by our sense of beauty.

All of the first four modes of intentionality overlap and interpenetrate; and it is only artificially that we isolate each of them. Nevertheless, we may set the aesthetic pattern momentarily apart from the others by virtue of its interest in the sheer "appearance" of things. For the aesthetic sense the object of interest is totally contained in its appearance, not in its use or function nor in its appeal to theoretical intelligence. The work of art, as such, exhausts itself in its appearance. It does not try to solve problems. It simply confronts us with patterns of sound, color or proportion. It may incidentally affect us sentiently by evoking certain moods and stimulating us to recall specific feelings. Or it may indirectly arouse moral concern. We may be able to fit a work of art into a story or into some theory. But essentially the work of art appeals to a distinct mode of consciousness whose prime interest is balance, proportion, harmony of light or sound, color, etc.

When people respond to a religious vision they do so vigorously only when its modes of expression have aesthetic appeal. Since the aesthetic form of interest is so powerful, individuals instinctively recoil from religious rites and language that they find artistically sterile. In many instances antipathy to religious life is the result of implicit aesthetic disillusionment rather than intellectual or moral discontent. And the adhesive that binds many people to a specific religious tradition may be, to a large extent, an appreciation of the latter's artistic expression of religious themes.[22]

But we must be careful to distinguish the religious from the aesthetic. The relationship of religion to art has been the subject of much discussion. Religious feeling is inevitably expressed in forms that can be looked at from a purely aesthetic standpoint, thereby missing their religious bearing. Ritual movement, poetic utterance, and the use of numerous symbols already ingredient in a culture's aesthetic inventory suggest a mutual intimacy in which it is often difficult to distinguish religion from art. For this reason a number of writers have assimilated religious consciousness almost totally to the aesthetic field. Such a maneuver, however, disregards the subtle ways in which man's religious insight suffuses the sentient, interpersonal and narrative fields of meaning. And it also fails to distinguish between religious and aesthetic symbolism.

Religious symbols represent a world (the sacred) that does not totally exhaust itself in the symbols themselves. The symbols of religious man always point beyond themselves. Aesthetic symbols, however, imply no such distinction between form and content, between a profane and sacred directionality. What they express is fully contained in the expression itself. As Susanne Langer puts it, they construe a "virtual" universe.[23] Their objective as such is not to conceal or reveal the sacred, even though by way of religious intuition they may be made into, or constituted as, religious symbols just as any profane object can become symbolic of the sacred.

We shall refer to these first four patterns (the sentient, interpersonal, narrative and aesthetic) as *primal*, that is, pretheoretical fields of intentionality. This is to distinguish them as a group from the fifth, which we shall call the theoretic pattern.

It is from within the primal fields of meaning that a sense of the sacred first took hold of religious man's consciousness. It seems evident that the sacred was taken as an unquestionable given in human experience up until the emergence of a theoretical approach to the world. The turn to theory appears to have distanced many of us from the proximity to the numinous professed by archaic man. The so-called transition from *mythos* to *logos* has made symbols and stories of the sacred ever more problematic for analytic thinking.

Whether the turn to theory is an enrichment or impoverishment of life is still being debated. What is often overlooked in this dispute is that in spite of the predominance of theoretical thinking in contemporary Western culture, the intentionality of most of our conscious life is still primal. We are still largely bundles of spontaneities, pretheoretical in nature. We are still engaged in the world through feeling and mood, through an instinctive interest in beauty, through moral concern. And, most important of all, our world is still able to be reached as our world only through some story. Primal, narrative consciousness has simply not been abrogated by theory. Story-telling, through which men express their feelings and concerns and in which they symbolize what they consider to be ultimately fulfilling and the ways in which to achieve "salvation," is an ineradicable and prototypical a gesture as are playing and laughing.

This is so even if we are theoreticians by profession. Professional thinkers, intellectuals, often make a great deal of the control over our lives that the advance to theory has made possible. At times there is even the aspiration to eliminate spontaneities altogether, to gain complete mastery over ourselves, and to eliminate altogether the antiquated, ambivalent "impulses" of the primal fields. Such an aspiration, of course, is itself rooted in a story emanating from the thinker's own primal, instinctive manner of being in the world.

Man's religious life, his myths of the sacred and his stories of God's creative and redemptive activity proceed originally out of the spontaneous movement of awareness touching on the narrative mode. From within the world intended by religious stories there is no question of the reality of the sacred. The sacred is a given. But from the point of view of theory such a "reality" becomes questionable, and stories of God often seem to be a product of some other impulse than the pure desire to know reality as it is in itself, i.e., objectively.

(5) *The theoretic field:* This pattern emerges in the awareness of a distinction between subject and object. It is a distinction not yet clear and self-conscious in the primal patterns. For in the sentient, interpersonal, narrative and aesthetic modes the knower is so united with the known that what later are called subject and object constitute an original, still undifferentiated whole. For example, in the sentient sphere "reality" is disclosed as so colored by one's moods, such as anxiety or joy, that it cannot be clearly distinguished from the sentient consciousness which apprehends it as such. Or in the narrative mode, through which feelings become "defined," the world is given through affect-stimulating stories into which the subject is so caught up that any "objective" distance would actually impede the grasping of such a world.

In the theoretic pattern, however, the desire to know the real leads the subject to detach himself in a deliberate, reflective way from the object known. He goes beyond descriptive and seeks explanatory knowledge of the world. Thus philosophy and science are born. The motive behind this effort toward theoretic detachment is precisely that of getting into a position to know the real *as it is in itself,* apart from any subjective moods, feelings or aesthetic bias, etc. Moreover, it seems clear that this move into theory is at least originally executed in obedience to the imperatives to be attentive, intelligent and critical. Thus the emergence of theory was inevitable given the dynamic nature of human consciousness with its need to know and inquire.

The question arises, however, whether such subject/object detachment is always capable of putting us in touch with all aspects of the real that the desire to know intends. Are there not certain instances of valid knowledge in which theoretic distance would be an obstacle to our exigency for the real? Granted that the desire to know must always be detached, need this detachment always be theoretic (subject over against object)? And does every type of detachment exclude involvement? We shall argue that fidelity to the mind's imperatives requires different forms of criticism in the theoretic and primal modes. Involvement in a story (religious or otherwise) has often been assumed by theoreticians to be illusory, simply because of the evocation by these stories of feeling, concern and aesthetic response. Our criterion of truth, however, must always be fidelity to the desire to know, not theoretic detachment. In the primal modes, theoretic detachment would be a frustration of this eros for the real in which a certain type of involvement might be a condition for its realization.

The theoretic mode of consciousness is most noticeable in the mathematical and natural sciences. The impressive results of the subject/object distinction in scientific knowing have led to our culture's (especially in the universities) adopting the theoretic pattern as the privileged road to the real. The consequences of this move are at the most ambiguous. Recently there has been a massive attack by some social critics on the enterprise of carrying the cool-headed, detached spectator approach (naively) associated with the physical sciences into arenas usually exposed by self-involving knowledge in the sentient, interpersonal and narrative modes. In these latter a rigid subject/object split is actually an impediment to knowledge. Cool-headed detachment is out of place when dealing with certain aspects of our world.

Thus there has raged a vigorous debate concerning the relative values of theoretic and primal modes of knowledge. There seems to be little point in denying that all sides will admit that they possess the desire to know what is real and that they want to avoid illusion. The problem does not lie here. It consists rather in the justification of the more radical option for one or the other pattern of consciousness as the normative one in which the desire to know unfolds. The scientist, for example, may appear emotionally detached in his work *within* the theoretic pattern, but he is anything but cool and detached in his choice *of* the theoretic pattern as essential for scientific knowledge. This leaves open the possibility that an exclusivist preference for one pattern of consciousness may be the result of capitulation to some other urge than the desire to know. If the preference for the theoretic pattern becomes obsessive in an individual or society, then this obsessiveness is not rooted in the desire to know the real, but in the desire for mastery or even a hidden drive for omnipotence. Any reflection on religion or belief necessitates an awareness both of the multiple desires of men and of the complex fields of meaning constituted by the several patterns of his experience.

The problem of the validity of belief statements revolves to a great extent around the issue of the primacy and hierarchy within the fields of meaning. It is especially the cultural and academic prominence of the scientifically theoretical mode that provokes a crisis of belief among countless educated individuals today. There have, of course, always been religious crises, usually tied up with cultural and social upheaval. But prior to the emergence of theory and science, most of these crises involved clashes within the primal patterns of experience. Certain symbols, for example, may have lost their power to mediate the "sacred" because of shifts in sentient, interpersonal, narrative and aesthetic awareness. And when symbols grow obsolete the gods die with them. Thus "religions" have come and gone ever since the dawn of human history as primal modes of perception have evolved and dissolved. An example of this is the tortuous transition from natural, fertility-oriented cults of Canaan to the historically centered religion of the Hebrews.

In modern times, however, a new dimension has been added to this tumultuous history of religious crises. While the timeless conflict of symbols continues at the pretheoretical level of human awareness, the questions which have arisen at the theoretical level have posed a more radical challenge to anyone who insists upon affirming the ultimate reality of a sacred realm beyond the profane, quotidian objects of experience. These questions apply in particular to what we are calling belief, the affirmation of the reality of a personal, trans-empirical, loving God involved in human history. Theory-influenced minds cannot help but ask about the value, congruity, and especially validity of the language articulating such belief. Such questions spontaneously erupt from within the theoretical pattern of consciousness that all of us, like it or not, have entered into to one degree or another.

To renounce these questions as inane or presumptuous seems to be a direct assault on the desire to know out of which they have arisen. As we have earlier emphasized, such questions arise in response to imperatives irremovably embedded in the mind. On the other hand it might be equally rash to hold that the answers to these questions (the congruity, value, and validity questions) await a purely theoretic response. For exclusive preoccupation with the theoretic pattern may itself be the result of a flight from the imperatives to be attentive, intelligent, critical and responsible. The contemporary bias favoring the subject/object mode of cognition may possibly be explained psychologically and sociologically in terms of perennial human tendencies to obstruct the spontaneous intentions of the pure desire to know.

It is my conviction that we need not be desperately troubled by the turn to theory from the mythic-symbolic consciousness that prevailed before it (and which still lives on beneath it). There is a decided gain involved in this move, for it seems to have taken place out of no less integral motive than the pure desire to know. What I cannot help being disturbed about, however, is the arbitrary suppression by theoretical consciousness of the cognitional capacity (the ability to mediate the real world) of the primal patterns. Once it established itself the theoretical mode has often been taken to be the privileged mode of cognition.

Paradoxically, however, if the primal patterns are to be rehabilitated today, and along with them the world of the sacred (which becomes transparent only in them) this can perhaps only be achieved by a consciousness that is also theoretic in orientation. Until the primal patterns are reinstated *by theory itself* as having legitimate cognitive status any reference to the sacred will appear gratuitous to many of our contemporaries. Such is the structure imposed by history on any attempt to criticize religion or belief today.

In part the following chapters will present a case for such theoretical reintegration of repressed patterns of awareness and the symbolic mode of thought associated with them. This book shares the concern of many recent authors that theory must systematically reintegrate the symbolic mode of consciousness characteristic of the primal patterns. I emphasize the term "systematically" because I am convinced that we are always unsystematically, spontaneously entrusting our awareness to the cognitive prowess of the primal pattern. Our sense of wonder still mediates our world symbolically. Symbols still shape our everyday consciousness, and these symbols continue to represent a realm of ultimacy that we seldom advert to at the theoretic level.

There is a disparity between our theoretic and primal appreciation of symbols. But there has not been, nor can there be, a total loss of symbolic consciousness. There has simply been a disastrous lag in theory's recognition of its own debt to the still extant realm of symbol. Most contemporary academic philosophers espouse the theoretic pattern as the only one in which the desire to know is sufficiently detached to distinguish the real from the illusory. What is usually forgotten in this quite understandable option is that the incentive to make the distinction between real and illusory is just as powerful in the primal patterns, even though the distinction is not made self-consciously. And it is especially religious consciousness, positing a distinction between the profane (ephemeral) and the sacred (the really real) that gives evidence of man's need to make the distinction between the real and the illusory, the essential and the actual. The "intention of truth" is no less alive in mythic than in scientific consciousness.

Where, then, do we locate religious consciousness in terms of the complex web of human spontaneities on the one hand and patterns of awareness on the other? In what drives does religion take root? What pattern or patterns of consciousness most suitably give it domicile? Or is religion in a separate pattern all of its own? And do we violate it by asking whence it originates?

One must proceed cautiously with these questions. The pitfalls are innumerable. But I shall contend that if we relate religion to the desire to know we may find that no one pattern of consciousness opened up by this desire suffices on its own to contain the phenomena of religious life. All the patterns of consciousness and all the desires we can identify in ourselves have some relation to religious consciousness. The task of the following chapters will be that of locating and criticizing specific manifestations of religious life in terms of the interlacing of desires and patterns.

In previous attempts to understand and define religion each of the five patterns has at one time or another been envisioned as the home base for religious awareness. Even the theoretic pattern has been given this role (especially in Enlightenment thinking).

Our point is that an understanding of religion and belief is least biased if it is formulated in terms of the desire to know rather than merely in terms of one or more of the patterns through which the sense of wonder spontaneously proliferates. The fundamental question today is not whether religion is most typical of the sentient, ethical, narrative, aesthetic, or theoretic modes of meaning. The most fundamental question for any philosophy of religion is that of the relationship of religion or belief to the desire to know which moves through all fields of intentionality. It is this question that we shall approach in the following chapters. In particular we are concerned with the question whether belief in God as Creator and Redeemer is ever in the service of the desire to know. And under what condition may religious awareness slip into obscurantism?

Summary and Conclusion

In the previous pages I have set forth what I think are the central questions with which a philosopher of religion must approach religious life and language. I have maintained that for purposes of thorough evaluation the phenomenon of religion itself may be situated both in terms of human desiring and in terms of the several fields of meaning through which the world is opened to consciousness. By employing these two points of reference, desires and fields of meaning, we can allow epistemological and psychological or other genetic questions to be asked alongside of phenomenological ones. The significance of this approach, however, can be only gradually unfolded as we move through the following chapters.

It is important, however, to set forth clearly, at the very beginning of this study, the two sets of terms that may help us to locate, classify and evaluate the various forms of belief and religious expression.

Working with these two sets of terms representing distinct aspects of human consciousness and being-in-the-world, I shall make the following points concerning the phenomenon of religion:

(1) To be acceptable by critical minds religion must somehow relate positively to the pure desire to know. If it originates out of any other desire alone it will appear illusory. It will have motives but not grounds.

(2) However, contrary to a prevailing assumption, the pure desire to know the world without illusion need not entail limitation of this desire to the theoretic mode. There is, I shall contend, the possibility of a pure desire to know which is self-involving, tinged with affect yet still not contaminated by other desires that may be operative simultaneously. My desire to know comes into contact with the real world not only theoretically but also through self-involving primal patterns of experience. This point will be clarified as we go along.

(3) Religious life (and language) is seated first in primal awareness and only later (in some cases) does it move into the theoretic mode. Because of its intimate initial association with the narrative (mythic and historical) mode of intentionality, and with the other primal modes, religion and its language are inevitably self-involving, emotive, concerned, entranced and, therefore, apparently undetached. Because detachment is so highly prized in the theoretic mode as essential for arriving at knowledge of the "real" world, modes of knowledge that do not share this ideal of detachment are often considered unreliable because subject to bias.

(4) At this point, therefore, I would emphasize the importance of distinguishing between and among the various desires that we can identify in ourselves both privately and socially. Although we have spent most of our efforts up to this point identifying and describing the pure desire to know, it is obvious that our lives are also influenced by other desires and drives. Sometimes the latter are present in such a way that it may be impossible to recognize anything like a pure desire to know as the central orientation in our private or collective existence. Each of our desires is capable of energizing the patterns of intentionality in a unique way, either shaping the world according to arbitrary preference or allowing it to emerge in the various fields in accordance with the desire to know.

(5) We must distinguish, therefore, between knowledge of the world from *within* a particular field, and the motivation-desire governing the predilection for or *choice of* a particular field or group of fields of meaning for relating oneself to the world. The dominant desire, for example, behind the choice of the narrative pattern of experience may be the will to meaning. Stories have the

capacity to keep one's "world" together in a way that theory does not. Consequently the narrative mode would lend itself readily to the expression of the desire for meaning. But at times, we shall see, the will to meaning tends to muscle out the desire to know. And then the narrative way of grasping the world leaves itself open to being energized by ambiguous desires and impulses such as the will to mastery, obsession with certitude, desire for security, etc. It is this fact that evokes much modern criticism of religion and belief. Because of the nearly universal use of the story-telling mode by religious communities, these constantly run the risk of story fixation. And those whose idealized pattern of experience is that of theory are quick to pick up any such fraternization between religious life and infantile or pathological impulse.

On the other hand, however, our distinctions allow us to observe and explain what we may call a theory fixation. Knowledge *within* the theoretic pattern may possess a detachment (subject from object) which gives the knower the conviction that his desire is pure and "reality" oriented. But the predilection for the theoretic pattern is anything but detached. There is even a certain amount of passion involved in the commitment to it. Any one or combination of desires may lie behind this commitment. I shall argue, for instance, that an exclusivist confinement of the "world" to what can be apprehended "objectively" may be the result of capitulating to a will to mastery or obsession with certitude. Somehow the subject/object scheme, while necessary for theoretical knowledge, also lies open to being utilized by other desires than the pure desire to know. If a person's or culture's objective is dominance rather than knowledge, they may fix on and fetishize the theoretic pattern. In this sense being theoretical is hardly being faithful to the imperatives of the mind. We shall expand on this point considerably in the following pages.

(6) We have at least implicitly made yet another distinction, between two types of self-involving knowledge:

(a) The type of involved knowledge in which the desire to know adjoins itself to the primal patterns as well as the theoretic one: realistic involvement.

(b) The type of involved knowledge in which other desires take over the fields of meaning so as to impose preferences upon the "world" inconsistent with being open, intelligent, critical, and responsible: illusory involvement.

(7) And we may also differentiate two types of detachment, one serving the desire to know, the second motivated by one or more of the other desires.

(a) Detachment in which the knower disengages his desire to know from other desires so as to allow it to reach its objective unimpeded: realistic detachment.

(c) Detachment of subject from object undertaken in order that subject might master the object out of some other impulse than the urge to know: unrealistic detachment.

These distinctions, while laborious, are essential if those of us who have been influenced by theory are to make sense of, and fairly evaluate primal religious attitudes and expressions. I think that I have made points here which are not always brought forth. The terms "involved" and "detached," for example, are often used by philosophers and critics of religion in such a way that "detached" means realistic, objective, neutral and unbiased, whereas "involved" means coloring the world according to one's preference. I shall insist that these words carry ambiguous connotations, deriving from a lack of clarity with respect to the distinctions between human desires and fields of meaning. I think the prevalent use of the term "detached" as realistic, and "involved" as subjective and arbitrary, stems from the view that the primal fields of meaning are purely emotive rather than cognitive, that they are fields projected by other desires than the pure desire to know, and that the pure desire to know the world must follow exclusively the theoretic pattern. I shall argue, on the contrary, that each mode of meaning, both primal and theoretic, is capable of being dominantly charged by any one of the desires we have distinguished. In this way I think we can allow for a primal knowledge which, while being self-involving and cathected with affectivity, yet remains detached in the sense of being uncontaminated by desires opposing the pure desire to know. So wont are we to envision the "purity" of our desire to know in terms of bloodless theoretical detachment that such a suggestion may seem preposterous. But I shall invite those who find such a suggestion preposterous to ask which of their desires they are allowing to surface in their own preoccupation with subject/object thinking. Thus the question of the congruity, value and validity of religious life and expression and its place in consciousness necessitates our attending to the complex fabric woven on the one hand from adjacent or intersecting desires, and on the other from the manifold fields of meaning.

Such a scheme, elaborate though it may be, allows for (1) a smooth assimilation by the philosophy of religion of a phenomenological approach to consciousness, (2) psychological or sociological critiques of religion, and (3) an epistemological interest in religious knowledge and language. In most philosophies of religion the epistemological question has been split off from the former in such a way that the questioning of the validity and logical meaning of religious language has been considered to constitute all by itself the "philosophy of religion." By situating religion in terms of desires we may return partially once again to questions of the origin of religious life as viewed by social science. By asking about the relationship of religion to the desire to know we enter the sphere of epistemological concern without leaving behind the question of origin or other questions social scientists might ask about the desires, urges or impulses from which religion springs. And by situating religion in terms of all the various fields of intentionality we allow for the data of religious awareness to emerge in a richer way than does a typical philosophy of religion that squeezes religious knowledge into the theoretical mold. Although the following chapters may not have the crispness and neatness that a critique would have which reads religion only through theoretical glasses, I hope that it will compensate for this in scope and fairness to the manifestations of religious life.

III
Religion and
Psychic Striving

At the core of every person's being there is an ineradicable "I want." From antiquity to contemporary psychology, authors have tried to give an account of the strivings of our nature. And to this day there is a great deal of controversy on how best to formulate the dynamism of human development.

Psychotherapists agree today that it is essential for our adjustment to life that we come to terms with the "I want." For if we arbitrarily repress it in any of its manifestations, we experience an internal division which leads to personality disorder. One part of us continues to utter the "I want." Another part attempts to bottle it up, for whatever reason. And this division of what limited amount of psychic energy we possess leads to a depletion and sometimes collapse of our native vitality.[1]

In this chapter we shall lightly probe the nature of this "I want" and the relation to it of man's religious life. Just what desires does religion respond to? We shall note that a case has often been made for the origin of religion in infantile needs. But if the central core of the "I want" develops from the bare need for security or gratification into a need for "meaning" and eventually into the detached desire to know the real, what then would be the psychological (and epistemological) status of the religious act?

Recent psychotherapy almost unanimously proclaims the necessity of our "getting in touch" with our deepest longings. We shall accept this suggestion as sound and clinically proven. In this chapter, however, we shall argue that contacting and appropriating one's deep-seated desire to know is both epistemologically and psychologically essential to our well-being.

51

We shall make two main points. First, religion responds to some desire or desires. Otherwise persons would not associate themselves with it. Undeniably religion issues from the "I want." It would be incongruous did it not "fit" some longing. It would not arouse excitement and expectations unless it appealed to some potent inner urge or urges. Second, however, unless it is apparent that the longings which religion responds to include the pure desire to know, there is little point in trying to defend religious claims against the charge that they may be projected fulfillment of infantile wishes, or what Freud calls illusions.[2] Any other wants, such as those for pleasure, power and even meaning are capable in principle of giving rise to illusions. Wishful thinking is an inevitability whenever one accepts something out of these motives alone. Only what we have identified as the pure desire to know intends to put us adequately in touch with the real world. For this eros has as its essential business the distinguishing of what is real from what is illusory. It is a desire that by its very nature has no satisfaction unless it achieves some measure of success in authenticating the real. Other desires do not have this immediate interest. Illusions can quite adequately satiate the needs for security or power; and to a degree, illusions can momentarily stave off the hunger for meaning. The desire to know, however, cuts through such pretense and exposes the illusory worlds derived from those orientations.

Is religious commitment in any sense a response to what we have called the basic drive, the desire to know? Does belief arise from that wonder which from its most primal awakening intends the real? Or is it mere "projection" constructed by sheer fantasy to satisfy some drive not innately concerned with reality?

Earlier we called reality the objective of the pure desire to know. This seems to be a much more adequate way of understanding the term than is typical of common sense and of a great deal of philosophical reflection. For these usually understand the real in terms of objects. And objectivity is naively understood as the result of seeing (rather than also of understanding and affirming) the data presented by the world. Such a notion of reality, however, does not correspond adequately to the structure of the desire to know. Being attentive (having good vision) is not enough to grasp the real. We must also be intelligent and critical. And we must also be open to the world in as many ways as possible. Reality, then, is better understood as that which is intended by the desire to know than as a mass of objects accessible to ocular vision tutored only by common sense and theory. Reality, understood as true being, is anticipated in our questioning and affirmed in our judgments. But it is not known merely by looking.

We are interested in the question whether religion is an illusion or a product of the desire to know. We may now define illusion as the fantasized product of any human wishing or desiring exclusive of the pure desire to know. It may sometimes happen that such a "projection" is later verified as faithful to the facts. But, regardless of such an eventuality, an illusion is best understood as that which is intended by some other desire than the basic drive. Keeping in mind these "heuristic" notions of reality and illusion we shall be in a position to assess simultaneously both the epistemological and psychological character of religious response. And I think we can do so much more fairly than can a purely objectifying approach to the "real."

The Desire to Know as a Psychic Drive

It is obvious that we are giving a privileged position here to the desire to know. By what right? After all, experts in psychology have given the status of basic drive to such psychic dynamics as the desire for pleasure, the will to power, the instinct for death, or the will to meaning. Seldom is the desire to know explicitly portrayed by psychologists as the basic human drive. Perhaps this is because in concrete human life the desire to know appears only precariously capable of establishing itself in the face of the overwhelming power of other desires. Freudian psychology in particular has emphasized the fragility of the reality-orientation of our consciousness.

In order for the desire to know to emerge as a distinct drive it has to become somewhat detached from other psychic urges. It has to assume a sort of purity and disinterestedness (which is not to say lack of passion) if it is to be differentiated from other desires. But since total detachment, purity and disinterestedness are unattainable in practice, the desire to know is often seen as epiphenomenal to or derivative of some social, organic or sensual inclination.

Still there has been at least some discussion of psychic proclivities in terms of *cognitive* needs. Abraham Maslow, for example, has presented instances of personal readjustment effected by allowing these cognitive exigencies to surface.[3] "I want to know," according to Maslow, is a powerful manifestation of psychic need, although in some persons it is more intense than in others. The so-called "insight" therapies seem implicitly to recognize a need for understanding and reflection in patients who have not yet come to terms with this need, and who therefore repress insights whose assimilation would be painful but indispensable to their recovery. Therapy in these cases consists of tuning into the lost frequencies of the mind's imperatives rooted in the desire to know.

A great deal of recent psychotherapeutic literature implicitly recognizes the need to know as a major psychic motor. But the most direct evidence of the possible priority of this desire over others may be gathered through the reader's own experiment in cognitional self-awareness. The evidence, if there is such, would have to be grasped by each person's own advertance to his cognitional performance. Undoubtedly, he has already been asking: is the desire to know a prominent human drive? Is it active in my own life? Of course the very asking of these questions comes forth from one's desire to know with its imperatives to be attentive, intelligent and reflective. So we can say that the desire to know is at least occasionally the dominant interest. And we might suggest that it is a drive which at a certain level of growth and awareness remains constantly prior to other drives, refusing to allow them to usurp its position. This may well be the deepest condition of freedom and self-acceptance.

We might note also that when a psychologist theorizes that the pleasure drive, or ambition, or the will to meaning, or social conditioning is the prime mover of the psyche, he does so, paradoxically, in order to satisfy his own desire to know. Thus the satisfaction of this latter drive holds priority over any other inclinations in his conscious strivings. Because it is as affective and fervent as any drive, the desire to know is a good candidate for the position of basic personal and psychic drive. I think I can safely assume that the reader will not question this passionately without by that very questioning verifying my point.

It should be emphasized once again that we are not placing the desire to know in any necessary opposition to other desires. Ideally all our drives mutually support one another. However, the recurrent condition of psychic conflict in the lives of all of us makes it essential for us to distinguish among the several leanings of our nature. And it leads us to ask: to which of these leanings can we entrust the status of dominant drive? Which one is the most surefooted in the maintenance and development of human vitality? Which one desire is most able to harmonize and integrate our other desires? Which desire best articulates the fundamental meaning of the irrepressible "I want?"

In highlighting the desire to know I do not want to ignore the importance of other desires. For these other desires are necessary for the very dynamism of the desire to know which enlists them into its service and employs them as vehicles of its intentionality. But it is also clear that alternative wishes at times deviate from the objective of the basic drive. They distract and seduce or otherwise counter the innately direct thrusts of the pure desire. Still, appropriation of the desire to know, self-acceptance in the deepest sense, cannot involve the repression or removal of the other desires but only their relativization. The freedom for which humans yearn does not demand the bottling up of the sundry manifestations of wanting. Rather it involves the search for the deepest core of the "I want." The closer this "I want" associates itself with the pure desire to know, the more do our desires approximate harmonious coexistence.

Facing Reality

As indicated earlier, the desire to know requires admission to all of the intentional fields in order to fulfill the first imperative. So we are not talking exclusively about theoretic knowledge (of which many people are not capable anyway). The desire to know opens out through all the avenues of intentionality. But it may also be frustrated in any particular field. The claim to know the world sentiently, interpersonally, narratively, aesthetically or theoretically may be ignored in various combinations of ways. For example, one may so exaggerate a single field of intentionality that the "real" is confined within its ambit alone. This reduction is particularly a possibility in the theoretic pattern. When a theory fixation occurs, then the need to contact, say, the interpersonal world may be thwarted, and the excess intentional interest diverted off into obsession with the theoretic mode of meaning. What is real then becomes limited to what is known objectively, in the naive sense of being "seen" by a cool-headed spectator. The interpersonal domain may then be disdained as unimportant, and the psychological consequences could be disastrous.

It seems, though, that the desire to know the real and to abandon illusion emerges most explicitly in the theoretic realm. There the purpose of knowing is to carry out methodically and scientifically what is done only instinctively in the primal patterns, namely to tune consciousness into the world in a *realistic* way. It is from within the theoretic field that the problem arises whether religion can help humans face reality, or whether it leads them to flee from it. Is not religious thought, a theoretician might inquire, exclusively the product of psychic projection of wish-fulfillment?

In order to approach this question frankly we must immediately recognize that the cognitive act most noticeably representative of religious awareness is imagining. And it is the intimacy of religion and imagination that raises the critical eyebrows of the scientist. Fantasy or other primal forms of envisagement may seem to be suggestive of escape from the reality of the empirically given, the "objective reality" of the theoretician. And it is because of his commitment to his own desire to know the really real that the scientist or empirically oriented philosopher often disclaims the intangible world of the "sacred" attested to by religious persons and communities. The sacred seems to many psychologists, for example, to be too closely linked to spurious mental faculties and functions to be accepted by one who wants, in all honesty, to "face reality."

Sigmund Freud may serve as an example of such a critique of religion. His example is especially illustrative because it is out of his own deliberate desire to face reality that he found religion defective and, in a sense, pathological.[4] His argument rests partly on his contrasting the "reality principle" with the "pleasure principle."[5] The latter is the postulate that dominates the mental life of the infant and, to some extent, the neurotic. It is the principle operative prior to the awareness and acceptance of the inevitable obstacles to unlimited libidinal satisfaction. The reality principle, on the other hand, is the premise which governs the mental life of the mature person who has become painfully reconciled to the fact that unlimited satisfaction of the pleasure drive is incapable of realization. One's own body, the outside world and other people combine to prohibit such inexhaustible gratification. They compel one to "face reality" and to forsake infantile illusions about one's possibilities in a civilized world.[6]

But the pleasure principle is never wholly eradicated, and so escape from reality is an ever-present possibility. For Freud the flight from reality takes the form of fantasy. Fantasy is the one psychic activity that remains totally in the service of the pleasure principle.[7] In fantasy one overlooks the harsh realities of life and constructs worlds for himself in which obstacles to happiness (which Freud, in contrast to Aristotle, defines in terms of pleasure) are imaginatively dissolved. And because religion relies so heavily upon fantasy it appears to be the very epitome of such illusory world-building. It is the antithesis of the adult urge to face reality.

Thus, for Freud, it would be preposterous to suggest, as we are doing, that religion may originate in the desire to know. Rather, he would insist, it arises out of infantile longings for security that should be replaced by or subordinated to the disinterested desire to know typical of the mature scientist.

The example of Freud is helpful to us because it illustrates how zealously a man can commit himself to his desire to know; and it shows how a passion for the real is capable of being the all-consuming personal and psychic drive constantly outrunning the competition of other urges. But the example of Freud's own scientific life also illustrates how easy it is for someone to subordinate all other fields of intentionality, through which the desire to know moves, to the theoretic one. And it portrays a prevalent academic tendency to limit the basic meaning of "reality" to what is apprehended from within that field alone. It has been pointed out more than once that Freud is a product of his own historical situation in making the assumption that scientific method is the privileged and even exclusive access to the world. And it was Freud who said: ". . . an illusion it would be to suppose that what science cannot give us we can get elsewhere."[8]

What is noteworthy in this brief portrait is the fact that a predilection for the scientific-empirical pattern by someone like Freud cannot possibly be itself the sheer result of a detached scientific thought process. If we recall our differentiation between human desires and intentional fields we may be able to clarify this point. The *choice of* the particular pattern within which one attempts to ensnare "reality" cannot originally be made from within that pattern alone. The bias of scientism favoring the theoretic pattern, for example, is not the sheer product of theoretic thinking, although the latter may attempt to provide subsequently objective reasons for its superiority. Rather the preference for a particular pattern as the privileged one flows out of human desiring. As such the enthronement of such a pattern is carried out spontaneously and unmethodically. This applies to the theoretic pattern as much as to the primal. As a recent representative of scientism confesses, the exclusively theoretic, subject/object approach is an "arbitral" choice, not one capable of methodically providing its own justification.[9]

My point, then, is that such a spontaneous preference may easily be made in deference to some other desire than the desire to know. Numerous modern writers have expressed the view that the option for an exclusively scientific delimiting of the real originates in the will to power, the drive for omniscience and mastery. If this is so, and it seems to be a distinct possibility, then we may conclude that behind such theory fixation there lies a refusal to accept the basic openness of one's desire to know. For one of the ways of obstructing the desire is to narrow down the fields of meaning through which it spontaneously flows, to disparage the cognitional status of the primal patterns.

What appears beyond criticism in Freud's approach is his deliberate consignment of himself to the demands of his own desire to know, wheresoever they lead him. He gives evidence of an unassailable confidence in the ability of this desire to arrive at its intended goal (=reality) if only it remains detached from other desires. Anyone familiar with Freud's personal life can easily testify to the courage he manifested in securing this detachment for the sake of what he considered to be the truth.

And yet, no matter how intensely one strives to be theoretically intelligent and critical, as Freud and the many who follow his approach certainly are, there still remains the possibility of inadequate attentiveness and openness to the world. The basic criterion of truth is not theoretic detachment but fidelity to one's desire to know, whose first imperative is "be open." Whether one is inclined to face reality or not cannot be measured simply by his theoretic brilliance. Reality may, after all, have aspects that cannot be known except through the self-involving, symbolic and imaginative intercourse with the world by way of primal intention. Fidelity to the pure desire to know, facing reality, may demand on the part of the theoretician a new look at the possible role imagination may play in opening the world to the reality principle.

Like the empiricist I would hold that the human desire to which we should give rein most liberally is the spontaneous desire to know. (It is impossible for anyone to question such a suggestion without tacitly giving it credence.) The urge to know is perhaps the only desire whose spontaneities I can always trust, even though I might shrink from following them because of vestigial allegiance to other impulses. Unlike the empiricist, however, I am maintaining that full surrender to the instinctive predilections of the desire to know involves entrusting it also to those primal patterns in which feeling, imagination and their sedimentation in symbols and stories are essential cognitive elements. I am aware of the rejoinder that I thereby relinquish the detachment which my desire to know requires as it strives toward its objective. After all, feeling, fantasy, symbols and stories all entail the passionate involvement of the subject in the "object" of knowledge. And whenever such involvement is a factor, knowledge is subject to being contaminated by biases leaning toward what the knower prefers rather than toward what is in fact the case.

I readily concede the danger of such bias. In the primal patterns, however, what is in fact the case, or what is a genuine possibility for being, cannot be known without personal involvement. (Actually, such involvement is required in another sense for theoretic knowledge also, but a discussion of this point would be too lengthy to undertake here.)[10] We must distinguish, then, as we did earlier, between an involvement that is in the service of the pure desire to know, and an involvement that attempts to divert the pure desire from its natural trajectory. There are both realistic and illusory forms of affectivity. Because of the modern exaltation of the theoretic mode of knowing, the degree of veracity in knowing has often been determined by the measure of detachment from feeling and fantasy, symbol and story on the part of the knower. Thus it is either denied or overlooked that there may be aspects of the real world that can be known only via the mediation of the primal faculties in which passionate self-involvement is a constitutive element. The lover's knowledge of his beloved, sensitivity to the sphere of moral concerns, awareness of one's role and function in society, and acceptance of one's limitations are examples of cognition requiring primal, affective mediation as a necessary condition for reaching the real world.

Insight requires various types and degrees of affect depending on the field of meaning. Thus exaggeration of detachment could be just as detrimental to knowledge as could overinvolvement. The pure desire to know must always be essentially detached, in the sense of being liberated from the privacy of self-interest. But such liberation requires as its condition an affective involvement in those feelings, persons, concerns, causes, etc., that open the knower out to the world in all its richness. Thus the criterion of detachment requires elaborate qualification when we are trying to determine the "truth" of knowledge within the primal patterns.

Is there, then, any criterion by which we can determine whether "knowledge" within the primal patterns, such as religious knowledge, is not mere wishful thinking or psychic bias? Since the theoretic type of detachment is obtrusive when used as the measuring stick for depth of knowledge at the primal level, how are we to know when we have the right feeling, when we are really in touch with other persons or are participating in a "true" story? We have already insisted, following Lonergan, that the fundamental criterion of truth is fidelity to the desire to know. But how is such a criterion to be used with respect to religious narrative? This question is significant because it directly poses the problem whether and how such religious stories as those of God, Creator and Redeemer, can put us in touch with the real or seduce us away from it. If their function is the latter, then religion and belief originate in some other desire than the pure, detached desire to know. And if our deepest, though often buried, psychic (as well as epistemic) need is the need to "face reality," then religious images and stories would have to be viewed in terms of pathology.

Or is it possible that religious imagination may be in the service of the desire to know? Can images and stories of God be so understood as to motivate one to accept the native openness of his basic eros, to augment its relentless passion for the real and its abhorrence of wishful thinking? If the religious imagination can motivate this radical form of self-acceptance, then it not only has proven its psychotherapeutic significance (self-acceptance being the norm of mental well-being), it has also manifested its truth-value in its fostering the interests of the pure desire to know (the criterion of truth being fidelity to this desire). Chapters V and VI will discuss the question whether belief is compatible with theoretic criteria of truth. In the remainder of this chapter, however, we shall be discussing the twin themes of how religious images correspond to what we have called the *fundamental* criterion of truth and simultaneously the question of the psychic value of these images.

Epistemological and Psychological Self-Acceptance

Even to suggest that religion can support the desire to know or the quest for psychic health will seem rash to some and ludicrous to many. For it has often been implicated with other desires whose interest is anything but the psychic expansiveness that accompanies a courageous concern for the real. Historians have repeatedly called attention to how religious images or belief in the stories of God have lent an aura of legitimacy to pretense, ambition and murderous hostility. And psychotherapists have testified often to the power of religious feelings and notions to barricade the patient against those insights whose appropriation is necessary to restore mental integrity. Because of the capacity of religious imagination to motivate the flight from insight, is it any wonder that both the cognitive and therapeutic value of religious expression have been seriously questioned? And when the challenge comes from those whose personal and professional lives are totally concerned with advancing human knowledge, it is a challenge all the more serious.

The questions we have been raising are troubling and complex. But we shall propose that the following is at least the beginning of an attempt to meet them.

Our criteria of cognitional and therapeutic value converge when the basic human eros is understood to be the pure desire to know. The degree of deference to the imperatives of the mind is the measure of epistemological integrity. But the degree of appropriation of these same imperatives is also one of the ways of determining one's status from a psychological point of view. A case may even be made that what goes by the name neurosis is often a kind of flight from insight.[11] Paul Tillich has shown how this is especially true of insights into one's finitude (awareness of having to die or the inability to realize all of one's possibilities).[12] Such insights, which strive increasingly to come to the surface of consciousness as we gain more experience of life, can easily be pushed back from entering into explicit awareness. But they can never be kept out of awareness altogether. And the uneasiness of the neurotic is evidence of his subliminal cognizance of repressed insights. His frenzied obsession with preventing them from rising into more explicit reaches of self-awareness is proof that he cannot altogether escape the exigencies of the basic drive that continually strives to open the world up to him in spite of his resistance. The imperatives of the mind also lead to the Socratic injunction "know thyself." And so self-knowledge and self-acceptance require appropriation of the imperatives of the mind in a special sense.

In what way can religious imagination be conceived of as favoring rather than diverting the process of self-appropriation? We have shown that this question concerns both the cognitive and psychotherapeutic value of religion. My proposal, then, is as follows: religious imagination advances the innate openness of the desire to know in those instances where it (1) reconciles us to our finitude and (2) awakens us to our possibilities for being. Reconciliation to one's limitations joined with a vigorous appreciation of human possibilities constitutes a quite generally accepted ideal of maturity and mental health. These two factors compose the core of self-acceptance. Consequently, in the ensuing discussion we shall be implicitly dealing with the problem of religion and psychotherapy simultaneously with the question of how images of God as Creator and Redeemer relate to the pure desire to know.

(1) The Sense of Creatureliness

By moving us to a grateful acceptance of our creatureliness religious images favor the desire to know, awakening us to its unrestricted, open-ended character. When they so function, religious images are immune to criticism because they themselves advance the free flow of our basic drive for more and more depth of insight and critical knowledge.

We must recognize that whatever enlivens awareness of the utter open-endedness of our desire to know, i.e., its unrestricted scope, is in the service of that desire (and is therefore beyond the criticism which comes from that same source). This statement, however, calls for further explanation since it will be vital to our argument.

Reflection upon my desire to know reveals that it intends as its goal everything that is capable of being understood and affirmed by judgment. Nothing is beyond its intention or outside of its objective. Thus we may refer to the desire as unrestricted.[13] Any attempt to fathom the possibility of something lying beyond its possible scope has already brought this "something" within the field of anticipated apprehension. So it is impossible to deny that the desire to know anticipates everything that is capable of being understood and known.

Everything that is capable of being understood and affirmed is equivalent to what we are calling "reality," or to what the philosopher calls being. The objective of the desire to know is all that is real. Therefore, whatever quickens in us an awareness of the unrestricted reality-orientation of our basic drive could be said to be "realistic," and to have a fundamental truth-value.

Desire to know, however, is not the same as actual knowledge.[14] Achievement does not coincide with longing. This is an obvious but most necessary confession. Such a statement would be a mere platitude were it not for the perplexing fact that we humans do not effortlessly reconcile ourselves to the gaping distance between our pure desire to know and our actual cognitional achievements. Under the impetus of some other urge, e.g., a primitive will to mastery, we may seek to circumvent the abyss that yawns before us when we measure the meager results of our cognitional attainments against the infinite horizon of an unrestricted desire to know.

Recoil from the abyss assumes a wide variety of defense mechanisms. The most direct way of closing the gap is to become desensitized to the unrestrictedness of my desire and to exaggerate my actual attainments. By covering up the latent awareness that my desire is radically open, I become less embarrassed at the poverty of my accomplishments. Or by overemphasizing the extent of my knowledge I shrink the field of possibilities for knowing and being. As I have already indicated, this lobotomy often takes the form of disparaging the cognitional competency of one or more of the patterns of consciousness.

Full appropriation of my desire to know, however, demands advertance to all of its elements. To pretend to omniscience is to blind myself to the element of unrestrictedness, and is, therefore, a refusal to correspond with my deepest wanting. Such a refusal has both epistemological and psychological consequences.

But in order to accept the distance between attainment and desire I need more than theoretic awareness. I need courage, the courage to accept my inevitable limitations. For behind the obnubilation of the openness of my desire there lurks a reluctance to become reconciled to my creatureliness. This hesitation takes the form of revolt against the distance between actual knowledge and the desire to know. Therefore, I may conclude that whatever motivates me to accept my finitude can reacclimate me to the unrestricted sweep of my mind's orientation. It can thereby place me again in touch with my deepest strivings—which is, of course, also a goal of psychotherapy.

The more I accept my condition as incapable of omniscience, the less will I be pathologically anxious about the inexhaustible extent of my desire. The less I strive for mastery of the universe, the more liberally do I release my desire to know and enhance the possibility of further knowledge. I then become more appreciative of the fact that I know something than resentful that I do not know everything.

Such is the spirit of wonder that religious images, like those associated with divine creativity, are at least at times capable of communicating. I am not attempting to vindicate the "objective" validity of such images here. Discussion of such theoretic questions will take place in Chapters V and VI. At the present, I am interested in whether an assimilation of such images in the spontaneous religious act is capable of corresponding to our *fundamental* criterion of truth, fidelity to the desire to know. And all I have proposed thus far is that religious images are in the service of the desire to know whenever they suffuse our consciousness so as to lead us to a sense of awesome gratitude in the face of the immeasurable depth exposed by our unrestricted desire. Religious images function in resonance with the desire to know whenever they motivate us to accept our native openness to being with courage and thankfulness. The self-acceptance that they thus engender serves the quest for both truth and health.

The multiple images conjured up by the religious sense of divine creativity may energize the desire to know by arousing at first in the primal spheres of awareness a grateful sensitivity to our underlying cognizance of contingency. This insight must be visceral and not merely theoretic. It must be accompanied by appropriate feelings and organic attitudes (correct breathing, relaxed muscle tone, etc.) which only the symbols of primal knowledge can communicate. Subsequently, too, it is possible for theoretic awareness to partake of the sense of awe originally awakened by religious symbols. "*Theòria*," says Hannah Arendt, ". . . is only another word for *thaumazein*; the contemplation of truth at which the philosopher ultimately arrives is the philosophically purified speechless wonder with which he began."[15]

Of course religious images are not required to bring about a naked sense of contingency, the realization that one's existence is not necessary. Contingency is experienced in one way or another by everyone. But it need not be accepted in gratitude. It may evoke nausea, resentment, indifference or bitterness in varying degrees.

What makes a religious interpretation of contingency distinctly and normatively religious (i.e., faithful to the desire to know) is the element of gratefulness.

Of all the possible attitudes we may assume with respect to our contingency, only gratitude appears to be capable of allowing us to accept and sustain the openness of our basic drive. Only the feeling that reality is a gift not owed is penetrating enough to allow the unrestrictedness of the "I want" to come into full view. The courage to accept the desire to know, then, is the courage to give thanks. And it is especially through religious imagery that a sense of joyful indebtedness seeps through the many strata of our consciousness, thus emancipating our desire to know.

Why is it that a *grateful* sense of one's finitude is the most congenial posture sentient consciousness can take with regard to the basic drive? Why does gratitude, rather than, say, indifference provide the atmosphere in which one can most readily accept himself as a knower? Simply because the essence of gratitude is openness. In gratitude, a person renounces stifling and neurotic claims to mastery or omniscience. He has a feeling that the horizon for knowing and being is inexhaustible. And by rejoicing in, rather than resenting or being indifferent to this openness, he freely lifts the restraints on his own desire for increasingly more depth of insight. Gratitude is the feeling through which the desire to know becomes a deeply personal desire.

If there is any single thread of continuity running through the countless and diverse human affirmations of the sacred it is the religious man's acceptance of his existence as a gift not owed. Even in those "religions" where the image or notion of a creator god is absent, there is still a pronounced invitation to thanksgiving. Some sort of symbolic eucharistic activity appears to be indigenous to religious life of all types. A sense of gratitude, we have argued, is essential to sustaining an awareness of the unrestricted aspect of the human desire to know. A joyful acceptance of one's creatureliness is required by our basic drive to insure free access to its natural objective, the fullness of being. It is in this sense that religion may fulfill the fundamental criterion of truth. Through its symbols and stories it has always had the potential for stirring man to acceptance of himself as a creature gratefully aware of his infinite capacity for knowledge and being, but humbly aware also of his inability to terminate his striving for more.

Although religious imagery may arise in this manner out of the desire to know, we must carefully qualify our conclusion in order to prevent misunderstanding. We are obliged to take note of those numerous instances where what goes by the name of religion has so saturated human minds as to drown any sparks of pure desire. The same images, stories and doctrines that motivate acceptance of the openness of our basic drive can easily lend fuel to impulses running counter to it. The need for security, the obsession with certitude or plain ambition have always appealed to symbols of the sacred for sanction. Some critics have even held that the greatest mass of man's religious life has been apportioned to the service of such ambiguous tendencies. Whether this contention can be historically supported or not, it would be naive to deny that "religious" imagination has played a major role in repression and oppression of various types at various times. Other desires than the desire to know have always competed with it for the legitimating power of religious symbolism. And it is this fact that explains the persuasiveness of so many critiques of religion and belief today.

The criterion of religion's "authenticity," however, is the degree of awesomeness and gratitude it manifests, that is to say, its openness. Any time religion becomes obsessive it loses that aspect which would align it with the desire to know. It then forfeits its fundamental truth-value at the same time at which it becomes neurotic.

(2) Religious Stories and Human Possibility

If reconciliation to one's limitations is one side of the conventional picture of mental health, realistic awareness of creative possibilities is the other. Thus far we have not dealt with this side of the picture. Our focus now, and in the following chapter, will be on the relationship between religion, desire to know and self-realization. We shall keep as our standard of psychic wholesomeness the same one that we are obliged to adopt for cognitional integrity, namely, "getting in touch" with one's basic eros, the desire to know, awakening to its imperatives and flowing with its trajectory.

Again we are not insisting that this is the only desire to be contacted. But in those in whom it is alive, becoming alerted to it seems necessary psychologically and not just cognitionally.

We have contended that religious imagination does not normatively interfere with the free flow of this drive. Rather it promotes an attitude favoring it. But can religious stories actually enlarge the content of our world? Is participation in such stories healthy and realistic? Do such stories present genuine possibilities for being, or are they mere illusions?

After all, we run again and again into the classic objection that religion tends to shrivel consciousness, to inhibit its native playfulness, its proclivity for toying with new possibilities. Many of our contemporaries have the picture of "religion" as a body of dogmas that have once and for all established the dimensions of the real. Religion for many conjures up feelings of stuffiness: the mere mention of the word leaves them with feelings of crampedness, of inability to breathe, of repressed sexual needs, etc. Can it seriously be held that religious imagination is capable of augmenting the actual content of consciousness? If so, how? The following chapter will deal more explicitly with these questions. So we shall make only some introductory comments here.

The role of religious imagination in opening up a world of creative possibilities lies in its refusal to allow the repression of the primal modes of intentionality. It is particularly in its use of the narrative pattern that religion may actually add to the content and scope of our worlds. This close relationship of religion to storytelling is something that will preoccupy us throughout the remainder of this book. The world of the sacred is set before human consciousness foremost through narratively symbolic thinking. Stories of what God has done or what God is doing constellate for a believer the "real" world in terms of which the "present" one seems vanishingly insubstantial.

But it is precisely in its imaginative, story-telling proclivities that sacral utterance seems to the empirical mind to be a shrinking away from the *real* world. How can religion be healthy if it is untheoretical and unscientific? Can it satisfy the desire to know being if it originates in the narrative mode with its concomitant freight of sentience?

Some psychologically oriented thinkers, who concede religion's positive role in mental health, have been content with Freud to call it an illusion, albeit a necessary one. Unlike Freud they insist on the therapeutic significance of religious stories, but they remain mute on the question of the truth-claims of these stories. It seems to me, however, that such ambiguity with its suspension of the question of the validity of God-language does violence again to the mind's imperatives. It makes psychologically necessary something that is epistemologically questionable. The term illusion, after all, usually implies wishful thinking. Illusory thinking is deemed responsible even though this involves backing off from "reality." Such a suggestion, to me, does not offer an adequate solution to psychic problems as long as it still involves an arbitrary suppression of the need to know what the facts of life are. Moreover, it raises insurmountable philosophical questions.

Because of the prominence of this psychological "double-think" and its immediate relevance to our present concern we might dwell momentarily on the ruminations of one of its most recent representatives. In a brilliant and fascinating book,[16] the late Ernest Becker concluded that man has a basic need for illusion. The question is not whether one can live with or without illusions but rather "on what level of illusion does one live?"[17] Becker might sympathize quite literally with T. S. Eliot's "human kind cannot bear very much reality." In fact, for Becker, as for his mentor, Otto Rank, neurosis and psychosis are precisely the conditions that result from seeing through illusions to reality. He quotes Rank's baffling variation on Freud:

> With the truth, one cannot live. To be able to live one needs illusions, not only outer illusions such as art, religion, philosophy, science and love afford, but inner illusions which first condition the outer. . . .[18]

Upon which Becker comments: "The neurotic opts out of life because he is having trouble maintaining his illusions about it, which proves nothing less than that life is possible only with illusions."[19]

Because religion represents for Rank and Becker the most manifest evidence of man's fabricating "illusions" to shield himself

against "reality" they are understandably excited about its psychotherapeutic significance. Both in its mythical and ritual aspects
religion is "a social form for the channelling of obsessions."[20]
Freud had viewed religious rituals as the manifestation in the
group of what obsessive-compulsive acts are in the neurotic individual. But Becker thinks that the compulsions of the neurotic
today occur primarily because the modern individual is often cut
off from the possibility of participating in the myth-ritual forms of
religious life, in which his obsession could be socially diffused.

Too much reflection, too much cold contact with "reality"
has produced the neurotic. He has bitten off too much, more than
he can chew, and his desperate attempts to cope with it have resulted in his agonizing symptoms.

> Beyond a given point man is not helped by more "knowing,"
> but only by living and doing in a partly self-forgetful way. As
> Goethe put it, we must plunge into experience and then reflect
> on the meaning of it. All reflection and no plunging drives us
> mad; all plunging and no reflection, and we are brutes. . . .
> The modern neurotic must do just this if he is to be
> "cured": he must welcome a living illusion.[21]

The way Becker presents his argument suggests that too much
alertness, too rigorous an adherence to what we have called the
mind's imperatives, too much taste for reality is pathological. Man
must buffer himself against the harshness exposed by his critical
urges, lest he fall into neurosis or even psychosis. The isolation and
emptiness of the neurotic can be overcome only if he suspends his
reflectiveness at some point and leaps, perhaps with a touch of
madness, into some "illusory" scheme. Traditionally such schemes
have been provided by religion, but the modern critical spirit often
prevents a man from taking the "absurd" leap into what could
save him from the sinful separation which is neurosis.

Becker's argument is an enticing one. It might easily convince
me were it not for what I think is its profound epistemological ambiguity. For in spite of his intentions, I think Becker remains an
empiricist at heart. His use of the term "reality" suggests a naive
realism, revealing his underlying distrust of the cognitional worth

of the primal, especially narrative, patterns of consciousness. He falls back on the word "illusion" to depict the worlds constituted by primal thinking because he uncritically gives a privileged position to the scientifically theoretic pattern in the task of disclosing "reality." Becker is only one of the countless thinkers who hold that "reality" is always somehow already out there "objectively," independent of the meanings of the subject. In this way of thinking, knowing "reality" always demands detachment, withdrawal of one's personal or social meanings, and gazing at the nakedly objective world without the mediation of any meanings. Such a portrait of knowledge, however, is naively modeled on ocular vision and it assumes that the knowing subject must be exclusively theoretic to know the world.

Sensing the pathetic psychological effects of such isolated, detached and bloodless knowledge of the "objective world," Becker understandably calls a halt to theoretic reflection. Given his epistemology, his uncritical acceptance of the primacy of empirical-theoretic thinking, he could not but use the word "illusion" to refer to that which would restore the circulation, the symbiosis between the subject and his world necessary for psychic survival. But, as it stands, he asks us to accept the value of religion without also nodding to its ability to put us in touch with reality.

W. T. Stace wrote in a similar vein:

> It has been said that man lives by truth, and that the truth will make us free. Nearly the opposite seems to me to be the case. Mankind has managed to live only by means of lies, and the truth may very well destroy us. If one were a Bergsonian one might believe that nature deliberately puts illusions into our souls in order to induce us to go on living.[22]

If we read the word "story" wherever Becker employs the term illusion, perhaps we could evade the epistemological frustrations to which his otherwise helpful suggestions lead us. Exhorting us to adhere to illusions, after all, is quite incompatible with what we have seen to be necessary to both epistemological and psychological integrity—fidelity to the imperatives to be attentive, intelligent and critical. Becker is not the first to suggest that psychic health requires participation in some fabric of meaning beyond the self. But in his and others' assumption that in order to so participate one must close his eyes to or repress elements of "reality," he is playing carelessly with a very loaded term. For most of us, after all, the "really real" world is the spontaneous one revealed to us by the myth or story in which we already participate. Without some story we would have no world at all, no "reality sense." The neurotic or psychotic have lost their worlds to one degree or another because they can no longer accept any story as meaningful. But the reason they cannot accept any story is not, as Becker implies, that they have had a privileged glimpse of the way things "really" are, apart from any stories. Neurosis does not stem from an overdose of "reality"; it stems from a failure or inability to follow the desire to know through the narrative pattern of experience. It arises from a lack of reality. The neurotic condition results from an inability or refusal to allow consciousness to unfold in the narrative mode required for apprehension of meaning. It does not result from an excess of reflection and criticism but rather from a failure to occupy a standpoint from which any animating criticism may come forth. Such a standpoint could only be provided by a world constituted by narrative consciousness. The mind's imperative to be reflective and critical is experienced in a distinct way in each field of intentionality. Being insightful and critical does not always imply being detachedly theoretical. In the narrative pattern being critical means being ready to revise one's story or "convert" to a new one. But it does not mean abandonment of the narrative mode altogether. This, however, is what the neurotic persists in doing. Often today his obstinacy takes the form of "fetishizing" the theoretic pattern, hoping thereby to gain mastery over himself and the world. Yet such mastery is maintained only by repressing the primal modes of structuring experience. And the world gained thereby is not reality at all but merely naked data unintelligible in themselves and unrelated to primal aspects of cognition.

The sentient, interpersonal and aesthetic patterns are intimately linked to the narrative pattern. Initially an individual's "neurosis" is apprehended as a malfunction of the sentient mode. The neurotic becomes aware of depressive states or of capricious oscillations of mood that make the world strange, unpredictable, and increasingly "unreal." His relationships with others dramatically change and he often experiences a crampedness in his ability to create or appreciate beauty. He is unaware that these transformations of his life are the upshot of a narrative breakdown. So he seeks to normalize his life by confronting head on the sentient, interpersonal and aesthetic aberrations. Such attempts remain futile, however, as long as the underlying problem of his life story is not faced.

Now it often happens that the clinically neurotic or psychotic individual is unable to accept the prevailing "reality sense" of others, and he may be inclined to look upon their stories as illusions. As we shall see in the next chapter, there may be compellingly justifiable reasons for his calling them lies. But this does not mean that pathological personalities alone have the privilege of seeing through to the truth. We should not have to make the schizophrenic an exemplar of fidelity to the mind's imperatives. For he too is under an illusion, the one which holds that there is "reality" for humans apart from stories. The neurotic is not facing reality; he is in transition, perhaps, between an outgrown "reality sense" and one more commensurate with his deepest needs and longings. But he is not in touch with an "objectively" real world that for the "normal" person has to be screened and censored by illusions. Only the most uncritical epistemology could allow for such a preposterous conclusion.

Reality, we have said, can best be defined as the objective or goal of the pure desire to know. But the pure desire to know is not exclusively the detached, disinterested one of the theoretic pattern. It is also the desire that calls for attentiveness, intelligence, criticism and responsibility in the narrative mode. But in this field of intentionality the precept to be critical cannot, as in the theoretic, give rise to objectifying detachment from the story-telling mode altogether. Rather it takes the form of retelling the story. To retell one's story, which, for example, is what psychoanalysis asks the analysand to do in its call for self-criticism, actually requires an asceticism and a type of detachment much more demanding than that of the theoretic pattern. One must detach himself from immature associations and suffocating transference if he is ever to continue his unfinished, broken-down autobiography. For there is no regaining a hold on reality, there is no revitalizing of the sentient, interpersonal and aesthetic structures of being-in-the-world until the story begins to flow again.

It is in this connection that religious stories can function to enlarge one's world so as to lead him to accept his creative possibilities. Although, as we shall see later, such narratives may also be appropriated in a pathological way, their normative function is one of allowing a continual expansion of reality sense, of the "world." Stories of God provide the context in which one can continually and critically retell his individual story without feeling that he is forsaking his past or moving into a voidful future. Christian theologians have shown, for example, how the awareness of a self-emptying, accepting God can allow one to remember and retrieve his past, no matter how filled with guilt or emptiness. Such a retrieval is indispensable to one's story. Trust in the presence and future of an accepting God allows the individual to tell his *whole* story, without repression of embarrassing episodes. It allows him to be fully attentive to and reflective about the multiple eventualities of his life while at the same time allowing him to weave them together in a continuous, integrated dramatic form. As I have already emphasized, the awakening of creative possibilities (the second criterion of psychic vibrancy) is contingent upon the pulsations of a living self-story. All the other modes out of which human creativity erupts are umbilically linked to the narrative one. In providing the context for an ongoing recasting of one's story, reference to the sacred, therefore, enlarges rather than shrinks the world constituted by human meaning.

Conclusion

Philosophy is not simply a body of abstract reflections gathered by uninvolved spectators of life. Although it may seem to have degenerated into this at times, the most lively and interesting moments in its history are those in which a *passionate* concern for truth stands out. And the underside of this concern, perhaps not often spelled out, has been the thinker's fidelity to himself. By that I mean his personal and implicit awareness and acceptance of himself as a questioner and his humble obedience to his mind's imperatives.

In the first two chapters I followed a notion of philosophy that holds its business to be, above all, self-knowledge, the self-appropriation of the knower. In this sense philosophy is the obligation of everyone who has entered into the theoretic pattern. Philosophy's goal, already implicit in the passionate search for truth, is primarily that of acceptance of and adjustment to the desire to know. This "getting in touch" with his basic drive is not something that one achieves automatically. It is a deeply personal act requiring not just intellectual ability, but what is more, courage. It is no easier for the philosopher than for anyone else to accept the radical openness of his desire to know. He is just as prone as the next man to devise schemes for skirting the inexhaustible depth which of itself the thirst for truth lays open to consciousness. The only difference is that the man of thought may devise more theoretically subtle mechanisms to shield himself against his native openness. One of these mechanisms is that of a theory fixation in which the philosopher disclaims the ability of symbols, myths, poetry, art, or interpersonal relations to probe the depth, to allow being to present itself to consciousness in primal awareness.

If, however, a person is truly interested, as I think he must be, in accepting the imperatives of his mind, he must be alert to those aspects of human life that can assist him and motivate him in the difficult process of self-appropriation. I have tried to show in this chapter that a necessary condition for aligning oneself with the transcendental precepts to be open, insightful, critical and responsible is a grateful sense of creatureliness and that out of such a sense the urge to face reality flows much more easily than without it. Therefore, it is in this connection that philosophy must look respectfully upon the images of the sacred articulated in narrative consciousness. For it is through involvement with such images that the sense of wonder is most inclined to flourish and grow.

Images of God as creative and redemptive, for example, are capable of conjuring up feelings of gratitude and the courage of self-acceptance that cannot be acquired from within the theoretic field of meaning alone. These can only be given to consciousness through a symbolic and narrative grasp of the world as a coherent, intelligible totality. The problems involved in such a grasp constitute the subject matter of the following chapters.

IV
Religion and the Desire for Meaning

The previous chapter portrayed the dubious results of absolutizing the theoretic pattern; the present chapter is concerned with the results of absolutizing the narrative mode in any particular configuration (the problem of story-fixation).

Among the countless desires felt by men, the desire for "meaning" also stands out as exceptional. Some critics would insist that this is a particularly Western and even bourgeois manner of focusing the polychromatic pinings of humans. They would urge that the question of the meaning of life is the product of decaying traditions, of marginal situations, or occasional crisis, and that the question of meaning does not arise in the normal course of a wholesome life. Yet there are others who insist that human vitality originates most characteristically in the will to meaning. Human creativity unfolds out of this impulse; and whatever threatens meaning threatens human life itself.

The desire for meaning must be distinguished from the need for gratification. The psychotherapist in particular is capable of bringing out the relationship between the two drives.

There is . . . a drive toward what may broadly be called, in a rather special sense, gratification. This is the pleasure principle. Meaning may be used to maximize pleasure and may itself provide gratification (as is especially clear in the arts). Yet the drive toward meaning is autonomous and distinct from the pleasure-aim. It remains a fact that sometimes we can purchase meaning only at the expense of pleasure.

. . . This drive toward meaning per se is reflected in the

clientele of the psychotherapist. The person whose life is gratifying although not very meaningful is not likely to come for
therapy. Nor does the person whose life is meaningful but
ungratifying come.

. . . The person who comes voluntarily to the therapist
is generally the one who is unhappy and who finds his unhap-
piness *without meaning.*[1]

Very few would deny that, if looked at in purely functional
terms, one of the purposes of religious acts and attitudes is to
endow human life with meaning. But what does it mean to have
meaning? Does meaning have any universal shape or features that
would allow us to identify it unmistakeably when it is experienced?
Is it really essential to vitality that our lives have meaning? And,
above all, can life be both meaningful and honest at the same time?

I am aware of the scope and complexity of these questions.
And I realize that they cannot be adequately dealt with within reasonable limits. However, in this chapter I shall suggest that we
touch them from within the lines of approach already laid down in
the previous chapters. Let us ask about the relationship between
the highly excitable will to meaning and the perhaps somewhat less
flammable, but still unquenchable desire to know. Our basic question in this book has been whether religious consciousness flows
out of the desire to know and helps it to reach its objective—
reality or being. Our contention has been that unless there is a
positive relationship to the pure desire to know, religious consciousness will today appear evanescent. If religion is indifferent to
the mind's imperatives then it must succumb in the face of critical
awareness.

Perhaps the most important question we can ask, then, is
whether the drive for meaning can serve the desire to know. If a
religious outlook is a meaningful one to individuals, does it also
satisfy their inborn interest in what is in fact the case? May it not
happen that the longing for meaning can become so exaggerated
that one may disregard the mind's precepts to be critical, to be
fully attentive to and intelligent about the realities of life? More
positively posed, our question asks under what conditions, if any,
the will to meaning may coincide with the pure desire to know? It

would certainly be an absurd world we live in if there were no point at which the desire to know converges with the will to meaning.

Before we go any further we must describe briefly what we are referring to as the will to meaning. The term "meaning" conjures up such cognates as unity, coherence and intelligibility, and it stands in contrast to the terms absurdity, chaos, emptiness, meaninglessness, nothingness, etc. The will to meaning is the drive to place one's existence within an ordered totality. This entails that the multiple episodes of one's life, that past, present and future, somehow hang together. Traditionally the patterns of coherence binding together the fragments and threads of a person's or community's existence have taken a narrative form. Myths and stories are the prime purveyors of meaning. One's life is meaningful if, and only if, it is part of a story. It is for this reason that religious consciousness has always used as its basic language the narrative types: myth, epic, drama, legend, parable, story, and varieties of historical, biographical and autobiographical accounts. The narrative mode arises out of a basic need to give continuity, climax and structure to the units of human experience. Religious story-telling in particular originates in the will to meaning. Can such story-telling also be a vehicle of the need to know?

I shall reserve for later a more extended and specific discussion of religion and story-telling as the embodiment of apprehended meaning. At this point I am concerned with a more basic problem. How does the will to meaning relate to the desire to know? An insight into any such possible structural or functional relationship will provide the base for our subsequent reflections on religion and story-telling.

The problem we are exploring may be set forth in terms of the patterns of consciousness previously outlined. Meaning or life-coherence is apprehended first from within the primal patterns. Meaning essentially situates itself in sentient, interpersonal, narrative and aesthetic consciousness. These modes of consciousness, rather than the theoretic, provide the vital, spontaneous structuring of the world requisite for meaning. Meaningfulness of existence is either present or absent prior to theoretical reflection. And meaning, as many psychotherapists will confirm, cannot be posited by intellectualizing alone. In fact, it seems that the spirit of criticism that we associate in a special manner with the theoretic pattern is itself capable of calling into question the meaning deposited in primal awareness.

Both collectively and individually the emergence of the theoretic mode of knowing is capable of precipitating a crisis of meaning. For theory requires a special type of detachment. And the latter entails a distancing of oneself from the feeling, involvement and story-telling in which "meaningfulness" is primally seated. When consciousness moves into the theoretic field, the imperative to be critical surfaces more obtrusively than before. And it is prone to turn the mind to detached reflection upon the stories, including religious ones, that have previously established the contours of our worlds of meaning. "Beginning to think," Camus said, "is beginning to be undermined."[2] One perceives, with the rise of the philosophic and scientific spirit, a giving way of the fertile soil provided by the symbols and myths in which awareness has previously been nurtured. The detached and isolated scientific subject easily severs his explicit consciousness from the pulsating tissue of the primal patterns.

This rupture seems to occur out of a reproachless subservience to the pure desire to know. "Facing reality" is the alleged motive for abandonment of what one has previously found meaningful. The symbols and stories that have meshed so readily with sentient or narrative consciousness are subjected by theory to an unaccustomed questioning that jolts them out of the pockets they have occupied in naive awareness. And such probing seems to leave them enfeebled, withered. They tend, under criticism, to lose their power over us. They are now relativized whereas formerly they gave us "absolute reality." Feelings of emptiness and loss of perspective accompany the iconoclastic process in which one prefers to follow his theoretically detached desire to know instead of an apparently uncritical will to meaning and the stories through which it is given form.

One is forced into an agonizing dilemma as a result of the differentiation of his consciousness into primal and theoretic modes. After the birth of reason one still desires meaning but is anxious about losing part of himself (that part which emerges in his critical capacities) if he abandons himself unrestrainedly to its pursuit. Or else one wants to pursue the rigorous exigencies of his pure desire to know in the theoretic mode but is anxious about the possible loss of meaning.

From his infancy the healthy individual is fed on stories and symbols among which those expressing a "sacred" content are often dominant. But through exposure to the modern critical spirit he is compelled to ask whether such primal human expression opens up reality to him as it is in itself. He is fearful that biases have arbitrarily colored the world so as to make it a secure and coherent one. Consequently he puts brackets around his moods, feelings and perspectives for purposes of theoretic and methodological purity. But in so doing he renders "reality" so raw and abstract that it presents itself as insubstantial. Unless the world is known also from within the sentient, interpersonal, narrative and aesthetic modes it actually appears to be unreal in the sense of being desiccated to the point of vanishing.

And yet a gnawing awareness persists that the primal channels through which the world is mediated to consciousness are too easily infected with primitive desires that counter the pure desire to know. In the haste to evade such a threat, well-intentioned individuals might easily tend to shift entirely into a theoretical key and remain there. And the longing for meaning of the primal modes is subordinated or repressed.

Is there any exit from the psychic and personal fissures elaborated along the lines of this dilemma? Is it ever possible, in other words, that the will to meaning and the pure desire to know can be given free play simultaneously? It seems to me that this is a central question for the philosophy of religion. And it is also, incidentally, a question of significance to those psychotherapists who posit the will to meaning as a basic psychic drive.

In the next section of this chapter we shall be examining what some prominent philosophers and social scientists (operating obviously in the theoretic pattern) have concluded about the will to meaning expressed through religious acts and expressions. Such a discussion will give us the background for returning to the questions we have just posed: Can we find any meaning at the same time at which we bow to the precepts to be attentive, intelligent, critical and responsible? And can we follow the desire to know into the theoretic field without diminishing the role of the primal modes of awareness in the constitution of meaning? Can we still tell stories while being fully intelligent?

Religion and Alienation

A prominent group of thinkers, among them both social scientists and philosophers, maintain that there is always a personal and social price paid for being religious.[3] Religion answers the question of meaning, but in doing so always entails some form of personal and social estrangement. Anyone or any group of people who appear to have kept chaos at bay are suspect. For in doing so they have veiled a significant and vital component of their consciousness. It is more courageous to live in the void with fullness of faculty, some say, than to live "meaningfully" in a condition of truncated awareness—a quite different exhortation from that given by Becker and Rank in the preceding chapter.

How is it that religion, in giving meaning, continuity, legitimacy and coherence to life, simultaneously falsifies world perspective? If we may be allowed to conflate the position of the numerous writers who speculate along these lines, the reasoning may be summarized somewhat as follows:[4]

Men are possessed by an indelible orientation toward carving out worlds of meaning from the environing chaos that such experiences as suffering, injustice and especially death open up to consciousness. Sensing the precariousness of whatever meaningfulness might be constituted in the face of death and nothingness, they spontaneously seek to plant their world orders on ground that would be absolutely immune to annihilation. Such a ground is provided by the "sacred" (something "cut off from," totally other, eternal and unassailable). To our theoreticians, of course, the establishment of this sacred ground by religious acts is an adventitious maneuver carried out in the interest of a will to meaning rather than out of a disinterested desire to confront reality. From the empirical angle of the social scientist, for example, religion may appear as sheer projection. It appears to have provided an aura of sacral legitimacy that has prevented worlds from dissolving the moment they take shape. But viewed from this theoretic field of vision it is doubtful whether religion has fully satisfied a deeper human craving—that which bears the theoreticians along themselves—the pure desire to know.

Religion, the argument continues, situates inherently unstable social and personal lives within a framework established by cosmic and eternally sacral stories. These stories or myths are repeated anew to each generation, thus providing the basis for tradition, the continuity of communities in time. Religious narratives and activities allow the individual also to situate his fragile existence within a firm (sacred) context that rescues him from the abyss exposed by his experience of evil. In formulating the "why" of evil through what is called *theodicy*, religious affirmation allows persons and societies to perceive purpose in their existence in spite of all that besets them. For without an acceptable theodicy, there has traditionally been neither community nor achievement. Meaningfulness ultimately rests upon the religious answers to the problem of evil and chaos.

Again from a purely theoretical point of view (that occupied by the scientists and philosophers we are considering) any theodicy will be opaque. The reason for this is that religious solutions to the problem of evil inevitably unfold first in the symbolic, narrative mode. Their initial appeal is to primal awareness. The stories of a suffering divinity, for example, may be congruent with sentient, narrative and aesthetic consciousness because in these modes what appears to theory as contradictions can coexist without mutual exclusion. It is in the nature of primal awareness to allow for the coincidence of opposites. The Christian cross has provided a satisfying theodicy to countless people apprehending it at a primal level. It has had the aspect of what we have called primal congruity. But as Paul Ricoeur has advised, there is no smooth transition from spectacle to speculation or from theater to theory. And, because of this, theoreticians are confounded when they ask about the value and validity of theodicies that originally take root in primal awareness.

Their contention quite often is that theodicies give a sense of rootedness to people only to the degree that religion falsifies human consciousness. They are unable to see any vital compatibility between the impulse for meaning and the disinterested desire to know. Consequently, it seems to them that whenever worlds of meaning have been constructed and maintained in a religious atmosphere this has occurred only by arbitrarily suspending critical awareness. Thus they judge that these religious affirmations lack what we have called validity since they seem to originate in some other desire than the detached, disinterested desire to know.

Moreover, such theodicies often appear to the critics also to lack deep moral and social value. Religious projections of a sacred world give people the impression that meaning ultimately issues from a totally other sphere of being. But as we saw earlier, our theoreticians posit on "empirical" grounds that all meaning comes forth from a will to intelligibility rather than a desire to know the real. As long as man accepts the sacred as the source of his worlds he will not come face to face with himself and his critical requirements. He will fail to appropriate his own creativity (which has even given birth to the gods) and accept responsibility for what he makes of himself and his world. He will, therefore, remain estranged from himself and his work, failing to apprehend the moral dignity that accompanies a sense of radical creativity. Religious consciousness not only obscures the imperative to be critical, it also cloaks the precept to be responsible, to become aware of the moral exigency to create.

This brief summary should be sufficient to illustrate the view that unrestrained release of the passion for meaning is capable of alienating oneself from his inborn need to be attentive, intelligent, critical and aware of one's creative responsibility. The desire for meaning, according to our critics, especially in its religious expressions, estranges one from the deeper urge to know reality apart from wishful thinking.

Implicit in this critique is the assumption that the drive for meaning is impregnable to criticism by detached intelligence. It erupts from an involuntary unconscious psychic depth that is beyond critical control. Criticism is aware that worlds of meaning may be full of insight and genius. But do they and can they conform to what *is*? Are they realistic? The need for meaning may arise from partial obeisance to the imperative to be creatively intelligent. There is admittedly a great deal of genius involved in the schemes of meaning devised by mankind. But, the critics may well ask, is there a proportionate adherence to the enlightened mind's demands for impartial attentiveness to all the data of experience? And does the passion for meaning allow for full reflectiveness concerning the truth of the world-orders it conjures up?

An example may help to focus this most important query. C. G. Jung, among others, has stressed the *value* to psychic life of feeling oneself to be part of a dramatic process that receives its archetypal expression in archaic myths.[5] The basic thrust of his psychology and therapy, it seems to me, is to reinstate the narrative mode as the center of conscious life. Many psychic disturbances result from the isolation and alienation of our egos from the fabric of meaning that only narratives can weave. Consequently, if we will allow ourselves to be swept up into stories larger than our own fragmentary biographies a sense of rootedness and psychic stability may be restored. Jung would insist that the modern apotheosis of the theoretic pattern of consciousness has blinded us to the essentially narrative aspect of our being. And his own technique is to probe the latent congeniality to mythic thinking that all men share by virtue of their participation in a "collective unconscious," wherein dramas are being enacted that we have lost touch with at the level of explicit consciousness.

Jung's is only one way among many of retrieving the therapeutic potency of narrative thinking. Countless individuals, perhaps without articulating it, have vanquished meaninglessness by way of reintegrating their lives into the structure of dramas: mythic, religious, humanistic, naturalistic. But, in all frankness, are we not driven back always to the question raised earlier? May not something integral to existence be sacrificed when we relax our theoretic powers and immerse ourselves totally in the participatory mode exacted by the dramatic pattern? This is the question that Jung's approach raises. Stated more positively, is there a possible story that could embrace and encourage our critical apparatus rather than requiring its expulsion from our personal centers of awareness?

I raise these questions for the obvious reason that not every story in which personal isolation disappears is, in the final analysis, a humanizing or truly liberating one. Sometimes restoration of

psychic equilibrium or recovery of a "meaningful" sense of belongingness may be, from an intellectual, moral or social standpoint,
regressive. Jung himself was aware of the possibility of "regressive
restoration" as one way out of psychic conflict.[6] And it takes no
expertise to observe how a romantic hankering for the lost, outgrown patterns of childhood ritual and fantasy can at times provide
the most fluid exit from the messiness of adult existence. Thus, as
Fromm and Tillich perceive, meaning may be found, but in the
process the self is lost.[7] I think, moreover, that the word "religion"
often suggests, at least to certain individuals, such a regressive restoration. And for very understandable reasons the same individuals
suspect any and all of its manifestations as tending toward reestab-
lishment of primitive patterns of existence.

It is the obvious recurrence of alienating myths and stories
that evokes the pressure of much modern criticism of religion.
Even if having meaning implies a sense of reconciliation with self
and world, its possession is dishonest and worthless as long as it
entails the repression of the mind's imperatives. Such fabrication
of meaning alienates what is considered most vital by thoughtful
men. Our critical urges may be momentarily suspended but they
are basically irreversible. Thus, if being religious entails uncritical
saturation of consciousness in the narrative mode, religious life
simply cannot be appropriated without great uneasiness by critical
persons.

On the other hand it seems equally impossible to live indefinitely without a participatory connection to some story. Even those
who have tried it, like Sarte's Antoine Roquentin, or the characters
of Beckett's literature, continue to grope for the narrative experience all the while they are repulsed by it. The testimony also of so
many psychotherapists is too weighty to dismiss in this matter.
Mental and social health require a zestful vitality that apparently
cannot occur apart from anticipated goals which the narrative
mode imaginatively produces.

Furthermore, even those most vehemently critical of religiously narrative existence are usually themselves devotees of some alternative myth or story, though they are unaware of it. Often it is
the rationalistic story or the "myth of enlightenment through empirical intelligence"[8] that links "theoretically detached" individuals

to the psychologically essential primal patterns of world-involve-ment. Without being critically aware of it themselves, the em-pirically enlightened are capable of living with a deep sense of the belongingness essential to mental equilibrium. They are unwitting participants in a tradition and dramatic community of believers. It matters little that their explicit creed involves the isolating enshrine-ment of the scientific method. Their spontaneous existence still remains quite in touch with sentient, interpersonal, narrative and aesthetic structures. Someone who exalts the theoretic component of consciousness in his thoughts and writings has not thereby dis-tanced himself from psychically stabilizing participation in a story with its concomitant rituals. He has simply not yet become de-tached enough from his bias toward theory to recognize the hold that stories have upon him. I mentioned earlier that the option *for* the theoretic pattern as the privileged one does not originate in the detachment usually associated with knowledge from within it. Rather it is a personal choice stemming spontaneously from the need to participate in the world at a primal level.

I think it is for this reason that the problem of life's meaning is not a besetting one or even an interesting one to many a so-called empiricist. His primal belongingness to a community and tradition with an entrenched creed provides the anchor necessary for psychic balance. And his implicit trust in its fruitfully progres-sive unfolding in human history rests upon the projected story that structures his existence meaningfully. The question of life's mean-ing becomes interesting only when one becomes aware of threats to it. And in stable traditions and communities, like the empirical, such threats seem remote. And those who would release any chal-lenge to such a tradition often seem to be simply unenlightened. In order to confront the question of the meaning of his life, the em-piricist first would have to recognize the possibility that his stories and rituals may not have originated in the detached desire to know of which he considers himself to be a most faithful disciple. Such a recognition, however, is exceedingly difficult to induce.

The Desire to Know in Narrative Consciousness

Up to this point we have taken for granted that having mean-ing in life necessitates having a story. And we have noted in particular the meaning-bestowing propensity of the myths that constitute the original language of religion. We have asked whether having meaning always demands a suffocation of the need to ask questions, especially reflective ones. In this section we shall begin our response to this and other questions we have asked along the way. (Subsequent chapters will carry it further.) We shall do so by providing a framework in terms of which the narrative mode of building up one's world may be seen as flowing with rather than against the current of critical reflection originating in the pure desire to know. Our contention will be that this desire to know demands specific types of narrative involvement while it repels others. (Although further elaboration on this point will be given in Chapter VII.)

To begin with, we must go beyond the rather stark suggestion we have made about the contingency of meaningfulness upon story. We have associated the terms rootedness, belongingness, psychic equilibrium, etc., with the apprehension of meaning. But there is a troubling ambiguity in these associations. The critics referred to above have been especially sensitive to it. They have alerted us to the possibility that the complacent sense of rootedness and at-homeness provided by our stories can fail to pacify our resurgent restlessness. Possessing mental and social equilibrium may actually be a sign of absence of vitality. For in addition to the need for firm boundaries and intelligible structures to our world we also have a longing to break out of them occasionally lest we die of suffocation: a story, we have seen, satisfies the former need, but can it fulfill the latter? Only, it seems, if it is a story that continually impels us and our worlds toward a self-revision commensurate with all our deepest desires and needs. But is such a story possible or available?

The meaningful worlds constellated by narrative consciousness and its dramatic embodiment are essential to both psyche and society. Neither would be identifiable, neither could congeal without some such patterning. Because of this, even the severest critics often look sympathetically upon the religious expressions of cosmic or historic meaning. That religions have a stabilizing effect is unquestionable. But "meaningful" stability, as history has shown, is not capable of being an enduring end in itself. The restlessness latent in various social strata and in unexplored layers of individual consciousness sooner or later bursts forth. It then becomes apparent that vital forces have been excluded in the name of "meaning." As Ernest Becker laments after he has argued for the necessity of illusions: "It is fateful and ironic how the lie we need in order to live dooms us to a life that is never really ours."[9] And if symbols and stories of God have been prominent elements in the legitimation of such repressive, self-estranging meaningfulness, then a critique of religion logically becomes the first step in the restoration of vitality. Iconoclasm is often an expression of the return of repressed impulse. It results from a vengeful reaction to the confinement and obnubilation of deep human needs effected by absolutizing the narrative pattern of being and knowing in a particular configuration. It is the predictable reaction to a story fixation.

Understandably the initial eruption of these repressed needs takes the shape of repudiation of all stories and the traditions they represent. A significant amount of contemporary literature, for example, is anti-story in sentiment and style. Its underlying theme is clearly that of disillusionment with all given worlds of meaning. Such worlds are rejected because they fail to represent adequately some yet unformulated longings. For example, Beckett's characters in *Waiting for Godot* typify the tense but static tone of emptiness that necessarily occurs in the interim between the rejection of one story and the possible emergence of another. And Sartre's Roquentin in *Nausea* leaves us an unforgettable portrait of the desperate but futile struggle to tell his story.

Psychotherapists of various schools often refer, in a variety of metaphors, to a basic need to outgrow and transfigure the stories that have shaped personal identity. Such transformation sometimes occurs only along with tumultuous periods of conflict and prolonged emptiness and depression. What was once meaningful may no longer appear to be so, simply because one's horizons have expanded at the suggestion of some other urge than the sheer will to stable meaning. An incrementation of consciousness brought about by one's increasingly detached desire to know himself as he is, apart from social assignment, may initially precipitate a sense of rootlessness. The old stories that have previously grounded his existence simply do not express what one knows himself to be. An augmentation of self-knowledge may for a time be accompanied by what would be clinically characterized as neurotic symptoms. This symptomatic behavior, however, is quite ambiguous. It is, on the one hand, pathologically self-defeating. But, on the other, it may well be the sign of vitality, of the need to grow. The capacity for neurosis, absurd as it may sound, is evidence of the self-transcending vocation of humans.

Self-transcendence, I would say, refers to the ability to transfigure the narrative mode of consciousness in such a way as to open it up to the movements of the desire to know. We cannot live without stories. We cannot disregard the narrative pattern of consciousness by living in the purely theoretic. I have already indicated that some of those who take objectifying thinking as their exclusive norm do so only in the context of a community with its own traditions and rituals. Life without stories seems next to impossible. On the other hand, the desire to know puts all interpretative stories in question. Religious stories are also suspect, because of their propensity to legitimate psychic and social stagnation.

Thus we have the two horns of our dilemma. We need stories, but we also need to know. Is it possible fully to respect both the theoretic and the narrative patterns of awareness when the latter is capable at times of giving into desires that alienate our vitality as well as the requirements of disinterested intelligence? Can we ever arrive at a point where we can rationally say it is right and reasonable on the one hand and therapeutic and meaningful on the other to submit to a particular story? What would this story be like? In the remainder of this chapter I shall attempt to show theoretically the compatibility of story-telling and the pure desire to know. And in the following chapters I shall attempt more concretely to illustrate this congeniality.

The Critical Component in Narration

A deliberate allegiance to the narrative-symbolic mode of being-in-the-world is not inherently abhorrent to man's critical sense. Before the turn to theory men were not, it is true, self-conscious about their stories. But this does not mean that they were always uncritical about them. The critical imperative is as much alive in the primal fields as in the theoretic. The method of criticism in the former is one of dialectic and confrontation, of "passing over" to other standpoints,[10] and of testing their fruitfulness. It is not one involving the detached verificational methods of scientific procedure. It is a method modeled on interpersonal exchange rather than theoretic detachment.

There is insightful creativity and a vigorous type of critical reflectiveness, for example, in Hosea's retelling the story of Israel's emergence from Egypt or in Stephen's recasting the history of Israel in the Acts of the Apostles. Such criticism involved detachment from some form of story, but only by virtue of deep involvement with another. Being critical does not entail bloodless isolation from commitment to any perspective at all. Rejection of the critical precept in primal consciousness, on the other hand, takes the form of immobility, refusal to dialogue or pass over to other points of view.

Criticism today is automatically associated with the distancing of subject from object. Accordingly it is assumed more often than not that one cannot confront the "real world" through stories. This assumption has given rise to a swarm of problems, none of which will be resolved as long as theory alone is burdened with the task of mediating the fullness of being to consciousness.

How then do stories meet the mind's critical demands when they obviously construct imaginative worlds not accessible to scientific sight or theory? Granted that they bestow meaning on the sequence of time through which our lives move, do they satisfy the desire to know and the desire to grow? Granted that they give us a "reality sense," do stories give us being? Upon this question pivots any attempt to clarify the intentions and validity of religious discourse.

Any positive answer to this question necessarily involves including within "reality" or "being" not only actual but also "possible" being. Story-telling relates us to reality by conjoining our givenness, accessible to us through memory, with our possibility anticipated in imagination. But not only with our own private possibilities. The narrative mode of intentionality is so linked to our communality that it is revelatory of the world's and others' possibilities as well. There is an intimated point where my story merges with a universal story, and all of our private histories are chronicles of the quest for this point of contact. Thus the attempt to find one's own identity through story-telling is also part of the larger human adventure of reaching out for the possibilities of the race.

The limits of theoretic consciousness stand out most obtrusively in the clumsiness of its attempts to formulate our common future. Oriented toward the actual as it is, verificational thinking projects futures that can be no more than sheer extrapolation from the present. This is why the *science* of futurology is to a great extent uninteresting and unmotivating. It is based on an ontology that limits being to a field defined by the temporal present. "Possibility" would then be the mere unfolding of latent structures already actual but simply not yet unveiled. Because of its compulsive fixation on the "realistic" present state of things, theoretic consciousness is incapable of disclosing radical possibilities of being.

It is primarily through narrative intentionality that the urge to face reality takes us into encounter with possible being. We are not being uncritical and irresponsible when we allow our stories spontaneously to bring a possible future into the horizon of the present and past. This is what the mythic mode of thought has always done. It has placed the Actual in tension with an Essential world, the profane with the Sacred, the empirical with the Ideal, etc. Because of the modern exaltation of the theoretic pattern we have been led to believe that the empirically available is the real and the ideal world the illusory. But the only reality accessible to subject/object thinking is that which is available through a perceptive apparatus functioning in the here-and-now world of "cold, hard facts."

We are not obliged, however, to refer to the worlds mediated to us by stories and myths as mere illusion. For it may be that they originate out of the desire to know being (as possible) rather than out of the need for gratification or sheerly out of the desire for "meaningful" security. A story, it is true, may also be gratifying and meaningful. But this does not preclude its capacity for responding to the critical dynamism of the human mind. To the mature mind, moreover, a story will not be gratifying or meaningful unless it also expands the horizons of the real world by opening one up to the often painful challenge of new possibilities.

The viewpoint which insists that being critical automatically means being theoretical is itself an uncritical position. It originates in a compulsive desire to squeeze the entire realm of being into the category of the "actual," understood as that field which is accessible to verificational techniques. Such "criticism," it turns out, is uncritical if in fact the realm of being embraces more than that which is accessible to theoretical consciousness. And all our reflections up to this point have been rooted in the conviction that the primal patterns of consciousness, centered in imagination, have the ontological function of mediating possible being to consciousness in a way that verificational procedures are not capable of doing. Far from being simply a faculty for evasion of reality and thus wholly in the service of the pleasure principle, imagination is also capable of being solicited by the pure desire to know as it strives toward being as possible.

Imagination, it is true, is protean and pliable. Freud's reflections in this respect are valuable and they warn us of a troubling possibility: fantasy may derive at times from the need for gratification. Or as others have emphasized, imagination may bow to the will to power, or some other desire. Søren Kierkegaard, for instance, in *The Sickness unto Death*, reflects on the malleability of imagination in the grasp of a will to construct an impossible ideal image of oneself.[11] Such use of imagination refuses to recognize the "necessary" or inalterably given elements of the self and is, therefore, "unrealistic." On the other hand, without the use of imagination there would be no possibility of human growth or self-expansion either.[12] For the imagination as the cognitional element common to the primal patterns is that whereby new possibilities for the self and society are ushered into consciousness. And the enfeeblement of this imagination is the direct source of human stagnation.

Again, however, we must be alerted to the possibility that the gratifying affectivity associated with one's story may be so intense that the story is no longer a medium for enlargement of the self and its world. In such a case the word "illusion" may accurately describe how the story functions. And yet, given the facility with which imagination is seduced into the service of any and all human desires, we should by no means overlook its potential for facilitating also the flow of the pure desire to know as it strives toward the fullness of being. Being imaginative, under certain conditions, is also being critically intelligent.

We come upon perilous epistemological terrain, however, if we think we can specify what these "certain conditions" are by appealing only to theoretical criteria. For theoretical criteria are more oriented toward the empirically given than toward the possible. Thus, they often exclude the possible as somehow unreal. Much so-called "linguistic analysis," of which we shall speak in the next chapter, finds religious language obscure because such analysis is not capable of dealing with an ontology featuring the arena of "not-yet-being."[13] Only a theory of knowledge that respects the cognitional potency of the primal patterns, rather than arbitrarily derogating them, can allow for such an ontology as religious expression demands.

If theory cannot alone determine the criteria for critical judgment in primal, and especially narrative consciousness, how can we ascertain whether a story is the expression of some primitive urge destined to shrink the narrator's world or is instead the opening out into a larger world capable of meeting the deepest of human needs? I have already insisted that the effort toward theoretical detachment from any and all stories will not lead us toward some neutral perspective from which we can adequately assess the meaning, value or validity of a narrative mode of being. Such is a prevailing but nonetheless arbitrary assumption. Criticism of one's story or of any social story or "reality sense" is most appropriately carried out from within, not from outside of the narrative experience itself. The most that theory can do is what we are attempting now, namely, to recognize the ongoing, dialectic, self-corrective tendencies innate in narrative consciousness itself. The final two chapters will address the question of the possibility of participation in a religious story such as that of God, Creator and Redeemer, in such a way as to reject any suppression of the mind's imperatives.

Summary

In the previous chapter we raised the question whether religion originates in the need for gratification. In this chapter we have inquired as to its possible origin in the will to meaning. In both chapters we have continued to maintain that it is not possible consistently to defend religious awareness unless it also flows out of the pure desire to know and is faithful to the imperatives of the mind. But we have emphasized that it is unwarranted to suppose that every satisfaction of the pure desire to know must occur in the theoretic pattern and in objectifying language. The human sense of wonder is manifest in all the patterns of experience, and the appetite for being cannot be channeled exclusively into that of scientific detachment. Moreover the absolutization of the theoretic pattern itself occurs as a result of succumbing to the desire for power, omniscience or gratification rather than in service of the pure desire to know.

Finally, the question remains, what specific religious narrative or narratives could possibly meet the demands of both the desire to know and the will to meaning. The quest for concrete instances will require separate chapters. Thus, in Chapter VI we shall contend that a philosophy of religion must have as one of its main projects the search for a vision of reality that motivates the liberation of human desiring, in particular the desire to know, in the fullest possible way.

And in Chapter VII we shall discuss in more detail how belief in stories of God relates to the most difficult assignment given to the desire to know, that of self-knowledge and self-acceptance. Before we can enter into these questions, however, it is essential that we first treat the question whether reference to God may have any meaning to those of us who approach the world from the point of view of theory. The following chapter will be devoted to this topic.

V
The Problem of
God-Language

The question of the relationship between knowing and believing has sharpened in recent years into one of language and belief. Perhaps the prevailing style of philosophy of religion has been too narrowly fashioned after the contours of this question. But because of the prominence of linguistic concern in recent philosophy we must carry our considerations of the God-problem into the morass of queries issuing from this typically contemporary form of criticism.

Very simply stated the issue is whether the language peculiar to the so-called "religious" is in principle intelligible or hopelessly nonsensical. What is the relationship of the extraordinary language of *homo religiosus* and of theological usage to our ordinary language? If there is no relationship then it is easy to see why religious utterance may be judged to be meaningless. If theology cannot consistently specify this relationship then it may appear to be anchorless loquacity.

A great deal of the discussion surrounding the question of the meaning of religious language involves considerations as to what conditions must be met for any utterance to be meaningful. What constitutes sense and nonsense in language as such? It has been the preoccupation of "linguistic analysis" to address these questions. Because of the immense importance of the "linguistic turn" in philosophy and the social sciences, then, it has been inevitable that the language of religion and theology also come up for scrutiny and criticism.

The underlying issue is whether the primal utterance of religious language can make sense to those who abide essentially in the realm of theory. Working in the context of the problematic of linguistic philosophy, therefore, we shall be preoccupied in a theoretical way with the question of the meaning of meaning. In order to determine theoretically whether religious language has meaning, what it refers to or how it illuminates, we must gain some control over our use of the term "meaning." In order to accomplish this we shall introduce the notions of "horizon" and "conversion."

Philosophers of religion seldom speak adequately of conversion. Of course, they presuppose it, try to justify it or repudiate it. But the study of the dynamics of conversion in human life is handed over to the social scientist. Unfortunately this robs philosophy of religion of what may be its most distinctive subject matter—namely, the articulation of the act of conversion itself. Traditionally philosophy of religion has tried to remain outside of the conversion experience. It has attempted to render critical judgment on the language issuing from religious converts by struggling for detached, "objective" criteria by which to assess the value or validity of religious assertions. Our point will be that a philosophy of religion has as one of its basic tasks the thematization of successive acts of conversion. In order to accomplish this, however, it must take into account also the notion of horizon. We shall discuss these notions later in this chapter.

Religion as we have understood it in this book involves much more than language as verbal expression. Religion is a perspectival or attitudinal phenomenon involving the entire being of its participants. It is a condition in which men are drawn toward something of absolute significance that language refers to as "sacred." Their response to the "sacred" or to whatever is of "ultimate concern" to them is only occasionally, and by no means inevitably, linguistic. Ritualistic movement, bodily orientation, social involvement, ethical stances, and even serene silence (the absence of language) may all become "expressive" of an underlying religious concern. Thus, an investigation of its language is only one way to approach the extraordinary phenomenon of religion.

Nevertheless, in recent philosophical discussions emanating especially out of the Anglo-American empiricist tradition religion has been treated as though it is *essentially* a set of linguistic assertions.[1] Because philosophy in this century has become increasingly preoccupied with determining what is meaningful and what is meaningless in language it is not surprising that much recent "philosophy of religion" is reducible to criticism of the apparently assertive language used especially by Western classical forms of theism.

That philosophy of religion should be so narrowly construed is lamentable. Aside from altogether overlooking the perspectival and corporeal dimensions of religious phenomena, such criticism has often assumed that religious language is "factitive" and cognitive rather than "importative" and existential.[2] Moreover, it has failed to come to grips with non-Western forms of religious expression.

In spite of its obvious limitations, however, a linguistic approach to religion is most illuminating. Moreover, the meticulous concern for clarity voiced earlier by logical positivism and later by linguistic analysis, both of which we shall describe below, has been a healthy challenge to theologians. As a result of its encounter with the empirical concern of Anglo-American philosophy, theological utterance has at times been severely chastened, and theologians have been compelled to strive for greater lucidity.

In particular the question has been forced whether religious statements can add anything to our understanding of the world. If not, then what are they referring to, and what is their use or function? Is it the implicit intention of religious propositions to give us information; or is the primary meaning of religious assertions to announce allegiance to a set of moral principles?[3] Is religious language merely the verbal expression of emotive commitment to a way of life, and nothing more than this? The linguistic emphasis has precipitated a flurry of attempts on the part of theologians to locate the place of God-talk or any reference to the "sacred" within the sphere of intelligent discourse.

The problem presented to theologians or philosophers of religion by the demand for language-clarification may be expressed as follows: Is the *question* of God itself possible? Before inquiry about the meaningfulness of statements it is essential to ask about the meaningfulness of the questions or of the problematic in the context of which assertions are issued. Let us note with many recent thinkers that a question cannot meaningfully be asked unless there is already given to consciousness some preliminary awareness of what is asked about. Questioning is always made up of a composite knowing and not-knowing. Because we do *not* know, we ask questions. But because we *do* know (something) we ask about "this" rather than "that." It is this prior, though undefined, awareness that gives meaningful direction to our questioning. Now when men ask about God or about the "sacred" at the level of theory they may be called upon to elucidate the prior inexplicit awareness that would make their question a meaningful one. In this sense the demand of the positivists and the linguistic analysts must be seriously considered. We must attempt to make explicit that which renders the God question possible at all. Otherwise we are vulnerable to the contention of the analysts that such explication is impossible because the question appears to be directionless. Can the preliminary awareness that gives aim to questions be intelligently and convincingly discerned or in any way "verified" in the case of the God-question?

(1) Linguistic Analysis: Verificational and Functional

The predominant philosophical trend in the English-speaking world of this century may fittingly be called analytic. According to this tradition the philosopher's job is not to prejudge, invent or speculate but rather to analyze and clarify the language employed by men who are always prejudiced, inventive and speculative. The distinctive work of philosophy is not to compete with common sense, science, ethics or religion. Rather it is that of setting forth the criteria for meaningfulness in language and attempting as far as possible to discern whether or not the languages of common sense, science, ethics or religion measure up to these criteria. Frederick Ferré gives the labels verificational analysis and functional analysis to the two most distinctive types in the family of linguistic philosophies.[4]

In the first phase of the analytical development that we shall call, following Ferré, verificational analysis, the attempt to formulate the meaning of meaning involved a lapse into what is now most often considered a naive prejudice on the part of these analytic philosophers themselves. Relinquishing their alleged intention of neutral analysis of the language employed by men, the positivists extrapolated a specific type of language, that used by the natural sciences, and set this up as the measuring stick for what is meaningful and what is not meaningful in the language of common sense, ethics and religion. This was a violation of the best intention of the analysts themselves. Their purpose was to clarify language, to remove the "rubble" from it. But instead, as is commonly conceded by analytic philosophers today, the founding fathers fell into the trap of saturating themselves with, rather than elucidating thoroughly, the language of science. Following a cultural and intellectual trend toward scientism, they understood meaning in the same way in which they thought the scientist understands meaning, i.e., in terms of empirically verifiable facts. The famous "verification principle"[5] held that a statement has *meaning* only if that to which it refers is discernible as "factual," in the sense of being accessible to observation. Aside from the logical problem as to what constitutes a "fact," the fundamental problem in this notion of meaning is that it assumes (ironically without verification) that the same type of observational or empirical elements constitutive of scientific meaning are required in the language of common sense, ethics and religion if these are to have meaning.

The attractiveness of the clearheaded and parsimonious language of science is still felt whenever we find ourselves attempting to clarify the meaning of statements by "looking" for their referents. That language should have as its essential business the asserting or denying of facts (as scientifically understood) is not only the conviction of the early Ludwig Wittgenstein[6] or of Bertrand Russell.[7] It remains to this day an enticing ideal for many of those who seek clarity and certitude about the convictions according to which they would live their lives.

Among the various types of language articulating such convictions is that which we call religious. Indeed religion comes to expression as language of commitment to something or someone of ultimate concern. And the language takes the form of talk about God or the sacred. Before we encounter the second phase of the analytic movement (functional analysis) we might profitably consider the problem of meaning as posed by verificational analysis.

We must distinguish here between two broad meanings of "meaning." Religious language attempts to express the "meaning" of its devotees' lives in the sense of articulating the "purpose" or "significance" of their existence. It attempts to answer what may be called an existential question: whether the individual's life or human history is absurd or not. It usually does so by the use of symbols and stories through which something of universal and ultimate significance is allegedly grasped. The expression "Divine Love," for example, may evoke the religious response of feeling accepted and secure in spite of evil, chaos, and apparent meaninglessness. In this chapter, however, we are not directly concerned with how this existential problem of meaning is met by religion and its appeal to the narrative mode of consciousness or other primal modes. Rather we are interested in the problem of whether such symbolic and existential statements of meaning are logically meaningful. We are asking how we should approach the question whether there is an actual referent that would render religious statements meaningful.

According to verificational analysts the statement that God exists is meaningless.[8] If any utterance is to have meaning one must be able to point to its objective referent through empirical procedures. In the case of God-language such reference is not possible. As A. J. Ayer pointed out, the statement "God does *not* exist" is also meaningless since there is no way to determine according to scientific criteria of meaning the facts that would constitute an adequate basis for affirming or denying His existence.[9] Furthermore, according to later analysts, in order for any statement to have meaning it must be in principle falsifiable.[10] That is to say, one must be able to set forth in terms of facts what difference it would make if God did not exist, if he seriously expects the statement "God does exist" to be taken as a meaningful one.

Examine, for example, the following religious and metaphysical statements: "reality is intelligible"; "human existence is ultimately meaningful"; "man's history is influenced by providential involvement"; "the world is charged with the grandeur of God." Now, if we follow the approach of verificational analysis, the possible meaningfulness of such statements is contingent upon our ability to elucidate the "facts" that would warrant such ecstatic utterance. But the test that would determine whether such facts are available (and the statements corresponding to them meaningful) is to be able to state what facts would conceivably give rise to the contradictory statements: "reality is unintelligible"; "human existence is ultimately meaningless"; "man's history gives no evidence of divine presence"; "the world presents to us nothing other than itself." What are the facts that would enable us to opt for one set of assertions rather than another? Since it is difficult or impossible to imagine what facts *would* stifle the believer's conviction that the elements of his experience somehow hang coherently together, his language affirming the ultimate coherence of reality is, according to verificational analysis, meaningless. Religion and theology are not able to state clearly what difference God's nonexistence would make. How can they expect their conviction that God does exist to make any difference either?

Most patent in this indictment of religious language is the notion that meaning is contingent upon either empirical verification or falsification. It was inevitable that sooner or later the restriction of meaning to its scientific embodiment would prove dissatisfying to philosophers concerned with the polymorphous nature of human language. Thus there has emerged a second major phase in the analytic tradition, that of "functional analysis." According to its more flexible conception, the meaning of language cannot be narrowly conceived in terms of the methods and syntax of science.

Where verificational analysis wields a rigid yardstick against which to determine the meaning of all assertions, functional analysis provides a flexible tape measure which will, it is claimed, fit not only the plane surfaces of language but also its irregular contours.[11]

In this wider perspective, the social and organic nature of language is recognized. Accordingly meaning is defined in terms of the *use* of language in the total context of life, not exclusively in terms of verifiability as defined on the basis of a naive conception of natural science.

As far as religious language is concerned, therefore, a much more tolerant stance has emerged. The philosopher recognizes that he has no right to impose a scientific standard of meaning on the "language-games"[12] of religion any more than he does on those of ethics or common sense. Instead he should assist in the clarification of the language within each distinct field of usage.[13]

In spite of the continuing demise of the verification principle and the widening acceptance of a rich and complex set of language games corresponding to the diversity of life forms, the question still remains: what does religious language mean, what does it intend, to what does it refer? It might be tempting to resign ourselves to the view that the meaning of religious language is reducible to its *use* in a language game or to its function in a form of life. Undoubtedly religious language is functional and useful in the lives of religious persons or in societies. It may have the function of solidifying, legitimating, or challenging a social order. Or it may provide psychologically the foundations for a soothing existence for the individual. It may assist in the maintenance or criticism of an ethical code. But is religious language nothing more than functional in this sense? Is its meaning exhausted by its function? Why does it persistently refer to some "other dimension," something sacred, ultimate, transcendent? Is it merely for utilitarian reasons or is it also in the interest of making cognitional claims about reality, claims somehow independent of the various needs that religion *de facto* fulfills in the lives of its participants?

Meaning

We cannot offer response to all of these questions here. What we can do is broaden the notion of "meaning" beyond the boundaries within which the linguistic analysts have employed the notion. A. J. Ayer himself, a rigorous exponent of verificational analysis, recognized the prevalent ambiguity of the conception of meaning.[14] And subsequent analytic thinkers have not dispelled the confusion, even though a great deal of valuable and original thinking has resulted from discussions of it. We shall reconsider this elusive notion, then, with the intention of adding elements to its elaboration that have been noticeably absent in the analysts' own treatments. Equipped with a fuller conception of linguistic meaning we shall then return to the question of the meaning of religious statements.

Linguistic meaning has too often been approached as though it involves logical and verbal operations somehow independent of a meaning subject. We shall emphasize here that meaning is above all else an operation or a series of operations flowing out of an actively intending subject.[15] It is always concrete persons, subjects with minds, who mean; and a great deal can be said about meaning if we reflect on this fact. The elements of meaning include not only what is meant or how something is intended, but also the *act* of intending. There is always a subject or subjects *in performance* whenever there is meaning. And it is in the "subjectivity" of acts of meaning that we can disclose an ingredient of meaning largely overlooked by analytic philosophy.

Of course the verificational analyst may tell us that we cannot verify "subjectivity," we cannot refer to it in an objective way; consequently our supposed reference to the subject who means is meaningless! Or the functional analyst might casually consign us to the relativity of our own language-game, informing us that what we say about subjectivity and interiority may have no meaning outside of our own playing field.

We shall suggest here quite simply that both critics must mean something by their chastisement. They have performed acts of meaning. Moreover, their acts of meaning somehow issue forth from their own minds, from their experience, understanding and critical capacities. Their criticism stems from their desire to know and its imperatives. It is this latter complex of mental operations that we shall call, following Michael Novak's interpretation of Lonergan, "intelligent subjectivity." Such subjectivity obviously cannot in one sense be objectively referred to. It is not one of the usual objects of our experience, for it is that *by which* objects are referred to and facts verified. Nevertheless, subjectivity cannot be called less than real simply because it does not fall among the ordinary "objects" of knowledge. In a sense, intelligent subjectivity is more than the externally real or "factual" for it holds the very norms of what may be called objectively real or factual. It is intelligent subjectivity that determines what is a fact and what is not. Nor can "subjectivity" be relegated to a "useful fiction" within the context of our language-game. For the functional analyst has implicitly appealed to his own intentional and critical "subjectivity" in the very *act* of criticizing our procedures. We contend therefore that intelligent subjectivity as an active source of meaning may also be "referred to," may also be "meant," even though it is neither objective in the scientist's sense nor merely a "useful" linguistic device. In other words it is meaningful to use language about subjectivity since the latter is a factual, though not observable, source of acts of meaning. Subjectivity need not constitute an aporia simply because of its immediacy. For, as we shall attempt to clarify, immediacy may be mediated. It is not beyond being meaningfully referred to. Subjectivity itself is a fact in a unique sense, and may therefore constitute an object of linguistic reference, albeit a unique one.

If it is not meaningless to refer to the immediacy of subjectivity, then, we need not hold that the verificational analyst's "factual" or the functional analyst's "useful fiction" exhaust the scope of meaningful reference. Intelligent subjectivity, by which the factual and functional are noted and understood, should also be noted and understood. What is really meant by, intelligent subjectivity, however, cannot be pointed to in this book or any book. Each reader, each person can grasp what is being referred to by "intelligent subjectivity" only if he reflects upon his own questions and his own acts of understanding and meaning.[16] He might find this extremely difficult. Perhaps he has never really attempted to apprehend *himself* in the *act* of meaning. Of course he has always performed this act. But has he ever paused to discern and understand what is going on in *his own consciousness* when he is attempting to understand the world? It is easy enough to get a vague feeling that something is happening, that there is vital activity occurring.when he knows or intends. But it may be an exacting task to distinguish and clarify the various elements of conscious intentionality: the underlying dynamism of a desire to know, the elements of experience, understanding, judging, deciding. It is an arduous but nonetheless legitimate enterprise to get hold of this "interiority" as a unique reality to be grasped, understood and affirmed as a "fact" itself.

We stress the importance of alluding to and grasping one's own interiority, one's own cognitional and intentional operations because we find in such reference to subjectivity a possible model for suggesting how religious and theological language purport to be meaningful. But unless an individual has undertaken for himself the appropriation of his own cognitional activity he will not easily understand how the theologian or philosopher of religion will attempt to establish the meaningfulness of religious language. Indeed there are numerous philosophers, and theologians too, who do not grasp theoretically how such reference is possible. Many have despaired of ever explicitating how God-talk might be meaningful in terms of any accessible horizon of knowledge. Before they have done so, however, they have usually already roped off the world of the subject as inaccessible to linguistic reference.

Most of the time our thought and language is confined to either or both of two realms of meaning: that of common-sense and that of scientific theory.[17] Within these realms reference to transcendence easily seems somewhat problematic. "God" simply does not fall among the observable objects of common-sense knowledge, nor does "the transcendent" disclose itself to those who have gone beyond common sense into the theoretical worlds of mathematics and science. Because the worlds of common sense and theory have seemed to exhaust the possible realms of meaning, religious language appears to have no place, no context, no horizon within which to have meaning.

What we have attempted to point out, however, is that there is yet another realm of meaning, that of interiority, approachable neither within the world of common sense nor in that of science, but only through the conscious subject's appropriation of his own cognitional and intentional performance. In order to apprehend this immediate world of the subject nothing less than an intellectual conversion is required.

Conversion and Horizon[18]

In order to appreciate what is meant by intellectual conversion we must introduce the notion of horizon. By *horizon* is meant the field embracing the totality of possible objects capable of being grasped or known from a particular standpoint. It is our standpoint that indicates where our horizon of vision or knowledge lies. And it is the horizon that illuminates the nature of our standpoint with its concomitant advantages and limitations.

By *conversion* is meant a radical shift of horizon. For most of us our horizon, the sweep of our vision and knowledge, has been determined by our common sense and/or theoretical knowledge. We tend to remain stuck in these worlds, often finding them sufficiently interesting and consuming. Let us recall, however, that for centuries men lived almost exclusively in the world of common sense, finding it quite enough to satisfy their innate desire for knowledge. And it was only by way of pulling us through a dramatic change of horizons that pioneers like Copernicus, Newton and Einstein eventually convinced many of us that the common-sense picture of the world is not adequate when certain new questions arise. In order to grasp what physics is about we have to suffer an internal mental readjustment, a change of standpoint so as to allow a new horizon to form. Through this shift we abandon the bias of common sense (that the sky is "up" and the earth is "down" or that time is absolute and universal) and we emerge disciplined and reconstituted into the new world of theoretical physics.

It requires tremendous effort and a rigorous asceticism to "convert" from sheer common sense to an enriched horizon that embraces both common sense and theoretical science. It may demand even more transformation of one's being to expand the horizon beyond that of common sense and theory so as to embrace also the world of interiority. The rewards for embarking on such a pilgrimage, however, are no less promising than those of the tortuous advancing from common sense to theory. One's own selfhood can be grasped in a new and revitalized way through such an exercise. Through such a conversion one becomes familiar with the source of the light that illuminates his worlds of meaning. Moreover, it is only from within this third realm of meaning that one can differentiate the first two so as to specify their real differences and prevent the confusion that arises when they are not differentiated.

One of the results of the intellectual conversion by which intelligent subjectivity comes into view is that the scope of possible linguistic reference is magnified beyond that visible to verificational and functional analysts. Both sides of the analytic family keep their discussion of meaning bound to the horizons projected by common sense and scientific theory in varying combinations. If meaning is a function of horizon, then, we should expect these analysts to have difficulty locating any possible referent of religious language. It simply would not fall casually within these worlds of meaning.

It is our horizon that constellates the realms of meaning for us. And it is also our horizon that determines what kind of questions we ask. Earlier we referred to the logical necessity of some preliminary awareness of what we are asking about as the necessary condition for a meaningful question.[19] We may now make it clear that it is our horizon which provides this inexplicit foreknowledge that invites such questioning. Without such horizontal perspective our questioning would be aimless, not real questioning, for we must "know" somehow what we are asking about even to ask about it. Consequently, the issue raised earlier, whether the God-question is theoretically a meaningful one, is seen now to depend upon whether we can disclose its possible horizon. In order to represent the question of God as other than aimless we must be able to allude meaningfully to the foreknowledge that would summon it forth from our questioning intelligence. We must be able somehow to grasp what the horizon of the God-question would be. And yet, to be consistent, we must emphasize the indispensability of personal conversion for entering into any new horizon. This is a point that is seldom, if ever, given full attention in discussions of religious language.

There is an almost insurmountable feeling on the part of many philosophers that the worlds of common sense and theory exhaust the horizon for all possible questioning. Because of this it is perhaps almost impossible in such a cultural context as ours to express theoretically what is involved in the conversion and horizon necessary for raising the God-question. We can perhaps intimate the possible difficulty of such development of consciousness toward a religious horizon by discussing the upheaval involved in conversion to one's own interiority, the difficulty of expanding one's horizon beyond the "out there" world of common sense and science so as to take the world of one's own self into fuller consideration. Only when such an enhanced horizon has been accepted shall we be prepared to advance a suggestion as to how to treat the question of the meaning of religious language. And, we repeat, such self-acceptance can be accomplished only by an individual willing to undergo an intellectual conversion.

There are many reasons why selfhood has not been fully appropriated into our schemes of reality, why we have not yet faced ourselves as intelligent subjects. Perhaps by situating the "real" in the "out there" world of common sense and science we have acquired a position and habit of mastery and power that we cannot painlessly relinquish. To include what we have called intelligent subjectivity in the scheme of the knowable and real might make our world much too unmanipulable. It seems impossible to get a firm hold on the realm of interiority by employing the techniques and categories we have become accustomed to in the worlds of common sense and science. Why not remain silent therefore about that which would challenge us to reconstitute our horizon beyond our ability to control it?

We should note, before proceeding further, that it would be a mistake to envision this self-acceptance in intellectual conversion as something that can be achieved by introspection.[20] The world of intelligent subjectivity is not appropriated by merely looking into oneself. We all have introspective moments, sometimes obsessively. However, introspection in this psychological sense is still carried on either in terms of common sense or science. It has not advanced beyond this compound horizon. Introspection objectifies the self. It situates it also "out there" in such a way as to gain control and mastery over it. Looking into oneself introspectively is by no means, therefore, an appropriation of one's subjectivity in the deepest possible sense.

The quest for self that we are discussing and encouraging here is not the objectifying scrutiny of one's hidden motives or unconscious impulses. Rather it is the adventurous heightening of the pervasive yet inarticulate awareness we all have of a basic desire to know. Prior to any reflection, prior even to any questions we are borne along by a dynamism that thrusts us toward the various realms of meaning. We are somewhat in its control rather than totally in control of it. Without any deliberate or reflectively conscious initiative on our part we find ourselves striving to understand, spontaneously interrogating.

Now let us abruptly ask the following questions: why do we ask questions? And how do we account for this enigmatic eruption from deep within us of a drive to know, of an impetuous need to make sense of things? Especially, how do we account for the curious fact that this drive to know is spontaneous and not a methodically chosen course of action? If the reader can *seriously* pose this sort of question now, we suggest that it is only because he has begun to open himself to a third realm of meaning, that of interiority. By thus magnifying his horizon beyond that of mere common sense and theoretical science he is empowered to ask a new kind of question. For it is our horizon that determines the sweep and scope of our questions. On the other hand if the reader finds the questions just raised to be aimless and frivolous, might it not be because his own horizon is filled out completely by either or both of the first two realms of meaning? A completely new type of question is invited forth only when there has been a radical shift of horizon. Such a shift of horizon in turn exacts a radical personal turn on the part of the intelligent subject. If an individual feels no deep obligation to ask whether the worlds of common sense and science are exhaustive of the possible realms of meaningful linguistic reference, then he would probably do well to read no further. For we are insisting that there is more to intelligence and openness than the mere accumulation of data within a fixed horizon. There is also the periodic experience of a breakdown of viewpoint and horizon followed by a possibly vertiginous sense of lostness as the first step toward constituting a more basic horizon. Perhaps the inevitable anxiety involved in such reconstitution of self and world explains our tendency to recoil from the challenge posed by horizon shifts.

What follows will make little sense to one who has not to some degree undergone what we have called an "intellectual conversion,"[21] the radical world-fracturing and rebuilding required to open up to questioning the third major realm of meaning, that of one's own intelligent subjectivity. But to one who has struggled to get hold of his own cognitional performance the following questions can be meaningfully posed, although we do not intend to pursue them here but rather in the following chapter: How do we account for and explain the *fact* of intelligent subjectivity itself?

What is it that activates the desire to know? What are the conditions that make questioning possible? Can we give any meaningful answer to the question why we have a passionate drive to understand? What makes us strive to distinguish between the real and the illusory, between truth and falsehood? Can we account for our relentless pursuit of intelligibility strictly in terms of common sense and science? What thrusts us so inevitably toward positing acts of meaning? Is intelligence a mere given, not capable of being understood? We do not at all propose to answer these questions here. We are merely indicating that they are meaningful questions to one who has broken through to the realm of interiority, who has dilated his world in accordance with the demands of intellectual conversion.

If the reader still finds himself questioning whether he has a desire to know, he needs merely to note that such a question has spontaneously issued forth from some such drive within himself. Thus, one can easily "verify" in an immediate way the "fact" of a spontaneous urge to ask questions. How can one intelligently "explain" this datum of the realm of interiority? Or should one abandon any attempt to become intelligent about the activity of intelligence itself? If we express the conviction that intelligence is out of place with respect to intelligence, however, we must remember that such a conviction itself issues forth from intelligence. We are strapped to our intelligence whenever we have any insight or make any judgment.

The exclusion of intelligent subjectivity from the subject matter of possible inquiry is the product of a dogmatism which proclaims that common sense and science adequately delineate the dimensions of the real. We have maintained, however, that intelligent subjectivity is also a datum worthy of understanding even though it obviously lacks the tangibility of what is usually taken to be real by common sense and science. We become aware of our cognitional performance not by putting a finger on it but rather by intensifying it. Awareness of awareness does not come by looking for it but by the heightening of awareness itself. We become aware of our desire to know not by getting outside of it and objectifying it but by adverting to our immediate immersion in its dynamism.

And we can discipline ourselves to recognize its presence even if we cannot focus on it.[22]

Now the point we are trying to make here is a quite simple one, though in the light of the still prevailing positivist mood it has required some rather tortuous introduction. Let us recall that the modern challenge to the alleged meaningfulness of religious and theological language stems from quite definite formulations of "meaning." Meaning is arrived at by empirical observation according to the verification principle. Or it is determined by *usage* according to a less positivistic linguistic analysis. Now in our reference to intelligent subjectivity we have disclosed a realm of meaning that is grasped neither by empirical verification nor as a strictly linguistic fiction. Subjectivity is an immediate datum that can be mediated to reflective consciousness and referred to as a most significant element of the real world.

Reference to the immediacy of subjectivity provides a model by which a theologian may attempt at the level of theory to explain the meaningfulness of religious language that already has meaning at a primal level to many people. Like intelligent subjectivity, the immediacy of God of which religions speak—so the theologian or philosopher might say—is not a datum "out there." God is not an object among objects, a fact among facts. Like intelligent subjectivity, divine transcendence may be understood as a fact *by which*, or *in virtue of which* our ordinary awareness and knowledge occur. Like interiority, God need not be referred to as an object of common sense and science. Like the subjectivity out of which these two worlds of meaning are engendered, the divine may be grasped essentially as illuminating rather than as illuminated.

The realm of subjectivity is a slippery one to get hold of. In fact, one simply cannot apprehend it in a controlling sort of way. For subjectivity is required to know subjectivity. It is both the knowing and the known. And the knowing can never be totally included within the known. Thus, subjectivity, continually transcending itself, evades full disclosure by objectifying thought.

This self-reflection may give us an idea as to why reference to God also appears so elusive and slippery to theory. Like one's own interiority, the theologian might suggest, one cannot gain an intellectual mastery over the transcendent. If it is so difficult to focus on one's selfhood, one might expect the same with reference to that immediacy which religious language testifies is closer to us than we are to ourselves. If it is so difficult to find language with which to mediate the immediacy of one's own subjectivity, then we may grasp why language about divine transcendence would involve no little struggle for theoretical clarity. Yet just as reference to one's own interiority can be meaningfully made, so also reference to transcendent being need not a priori be called meaningless, simply because of the struggle it involves or simply because it resists intellectual and linguistic mastery. It is not merely the focused upon that is to be called linguistically meaningful. That in virtue of which our focusing occurs can also be talked about, provided that our horizon expands sufficiently. Such horizon expansion, however, always requires what we have called conversion.

Some philosophers of religion would be inclined to go much further than we have gone here. They would link transcendent being and subjectivity together in order to respond to questions that emerge once the third realm of meaning has been constituted. Thus, they would posit a fourth realm of meaning, that of divine transcendence as the necessary condition of questioning, as the intended goal of the desire to know, or as implicitly affirmed in every act of judgment. They would appeal to the notion of the infinite as that which responds to the questions raised when our horizon extends into the elusive realm of interiority.

We need not pursue such possibilities here. The following chapter will be concerned with them. Here our intention has been essentially that of indicating what is involved in horizon enlargement. Whether language about God is meaningful or not depends upon what one envisions as the realm or realms of possible meaning. The latter in turn are constituted by one's horizon. The extent of one's horizon, in turn, depends in part at least upon the degree to which one is willing to risk himself. We do not often think of the development of knowledge as involving risk and conversion, breakdown and restructuring of self. We prefer to see knowing as a smooth and linear expansion of a given set of ideas based upon a fixed pattern of inquiring. Yet such a view of knowledge is both historically and epistemologically naive. Science itself advances only by way of revolutions through which great risk and courage is periodically manifested in the revision of basic paradigms and models representing natural phenomena. The insights of philosophers have often come at the price of great personal suffering. For, as Tillich observes, "Truth without the way [to the truth] is dead."[23] The self-knowledge toward which psychotherapy summons the patient involves an agonizing recovery of a willingness to look at the facts concerning oneself. In all of these cases the advancing of knowledge involves much more than the amassing of new data. Indispensable to genuine growth of insight and knowledge there is required at times both a convulsive rupturing of the surface with which one has previously been comfortable and the courage to risk foundering for a while until a deeper level has been reached. The acquisition of a broadened horizon involves radical restructuring of oneself. Resolve, maturity, courage, and knowing are more intimately related than we like to think. It may be that the theory-praxis of knowing that we are expressing here cannot be understood itself until one has personally and radically readjusted his previous way of looking at himself and the world.

Thus we make no pretense in this chapter of focusing upon any possible object of religiously linguistic reference. We are merely concerned to point out what may be involved in any individual's moving into a world whose horizon beckons forth the question of God, so as to make it an intelligible question. From our knowledge of what has been required in the shifts of horizon undertaken in ordinary expansion of consciousness, we cannot rule out the possibility that the capacity to accept religious language as meaningful also depends upon a "conversion" experience, understood in the specific way we have attempted to portray here.

In any case, such a transformation could not be formally put into words. One can neither see nor fully conceptualize a conversion; one must undergo it. This is why it is impossible to find some neutral ground from which both believer and unbeliever can assess the meaningfulness of religious language to the satisfaction of each other. One cannot grasp the import of quantum physics or the general theory of relativity until he has personally disciplined himself away from the tendency to draw vivid pictures of the natural world. One cannot appropriate his own immediacy unless he perhaps excruciatingly abandons the comfortable belief that the real is located exclusively in the "out-there" world of common sense and science. "Intelligent subjectivity" means nothing to one who has not experienced an intellectual conversion. Inasmuch as the "normal" development of consciousness itself relies upon periodic upheavals of one's world, the possible extension of the domain of the real into the world of religious transcendence would seem to entail at least as much on its part. To be able even to ask the question of God might first entail a radical breakdown of one's present way of looking at things. Such a breakdown, of course, will implicate what we have called the primal patterns of knowing. In fact, we might say that a theoretical readjustment of the world so as to allow for a transcendent dimension will probably not even be attempted prior to a narrative revision.

Moreover, Bernard Lonergan, from whose thought we have drawn much of our reflection in this book, holds that moral and religious conversion may be necessary conditions for undergoing intellectual conversion.[24] In order to include the realm of intelligent subjectivity within one's horizon a predisposition of openness is required. Such openness, I would add, requires the co-operation of the primal patterns. If one's life-story is a self-revising one, the continual conversions involved at the narrative level of consciousness may provide an openness of character that will also allow for expansion of horizon at the theoretical level.

Conclusion

The critic of language attempts to determine whether religious and theological expression is meaningful, whether it possesses any possible referent. The intent of this chapter has not been one of disclosing or describing that to which religious language points. This would not only be impossible, it would be contrary to our basic contention. For what we have emphatically proposed is the necessity of personal self-transformation as the necessary condition for continued appropriation of all the realms of meaning. A personal conversion is required in the shift from common sense to theory. Science means little or nothing to, and may even evoke scorn from, the man of sheer common sense. A personal transformation is an even more exacting prerequisite for appropriating the world of subjectivity. "Subjectivity" undoubtedly means nothing to the man whose horizon is filled up with the objects of common sense and scientific knowledge. For meaningfulness depends upon horizon. And breadth of horizon is somehow contingent upon direction and intensity of personal conversion.

The conclusion we have been working toward, therefore, should not be unanticipated: the potential meaningfulness of religious language also may be elicited only in terms of a horizon constituted through personal conversion. In the light of what we have noticed about the conditions for meaningfulness of scientific language, and the language of subjectivity, this conclusion should hardly be unexpected. Our appeal to the necessity of conversion as the condition for grasping or being grasped by religious language is not a *deus ex machina* contrived to remove religious language from the range of possible criticism. Instead our accentuation of the notion of conversion is intended to show that meaning in religious expression involves the same basic elements of development of consciousness required for the grasping of scientific meaning as well as the lineaments of intelligent subjectivity. Instead of playing down the significance of radical breakdown and reconstitution of horizon for grasp of meaning we should highlight it. An adequate criticism of the language used by men should not overlook this element of conversion and the restructuring of thought and utterance that accompany it.

Thus our procedure has in no way attempted to "verify" the existence of God. We have merely attempted to criticize the restrictive horizon out of which many analysts have issued their challenge to those who employ religious language. Like the language employed when we attempt to plumb our own subjectivity, the language used by religious persons somehow does not seem to bring before our eyes and minds anything definite to focus upon. And yet, because of their horizon, those who use religious language may be confident that it has meaning not only in the primal fields but also in a theoretical pattern open to the realm of intelligent subjectivity.

VI
Belief in God and the Desire to Know

Granted that belief in God may satisfy my desire for meaning; does it also fully satisfy my desire to know? This is the question we are left with from the previous chapters.

Why people accept or reject religious views and traditions is ultimately not determinable through logical analysis or scientific investigation. Because genuine commitment or refusal of commitment involve elements of will, hidden from any viewpoint (including the willer's own), it is impossible to disclose fully the motivation behind a "believer's" public or private intercourse with a religious community. The religious imagination is itself the vehicle of a basic orientation of human willing as well as of knowing.[1] And this makes any theoretically systematic study of religious acts less than adequate to probe their nonrational, primal aspects.

Still, while any particular instance of religious allegiance is impervious to exhaustive analysis, it is possible nonetheless to speculate in general on the relationship of such commitment to the human drives, needs and desires to which we have adverted in this book. Such speculation seems especially necessary if we are to determine whether belief in God (as we have understood this expression) can correspond to the pure desire to know and not simply derive from the desire for meaning. In this chapter we shall examine this question. It is a question that is usually treated as the problem of "Reason and Faith" or "Knowledge and Belief." However, we shall approach it not by comparing acts of knowledge so much as by exploring and comparing the intentionality of human desires. Specifically, how do we situate the "will to believe" in terms of the desire to know? I shall argue that the will to believe is itself not fully awakened until it merges with the disinterested desire to know. We have observed in the previous chapters the power and pervasiveness of our craving for intelligibility and we have also continually tried to bring to light the basic though sometimes buried need we have to face the facts that confront us in our experience. But we have not yet established whether or not these two types of longing can be fully concordant with each other. For we must continually ask whether it is "realistic" to seek intelligibility and meaning for ourselves in our world. Does the desire for meaning allow us to give full play to our desire to know, or does it seduce us into acquiescence to schemes arising from wishful thinking?

We have carefully distinguished between the desire for meaning and the desire to know. (The former may be insightful, but not fully attentive and critical.) And we have found the narrative mode, used by myth and religion, to be the one in which the desire for meaning primordially expresses itself. We must now again take up the question whether and how the narrative mode can also accommodate the pure desire to know. It has often been assumed that only the theoretic mode can give full access to the latter and that narrative consciousness is too easily possessed by other desires to be capable of being realistic. Behind the illusory reality sense projected by stories, it is often assumed, there is a deeper, objective reality to which our desire to know can penetrate only when it enters through the realm of theory. And then theory may find something that will show the reality sense to be a mere illusory covering.

If we are to allow for the possibility of a *realistic story*, one that answers not only to the desire for meaning but also to the desire to know, an essential condition must be fulfilled. It must be established that the objective of my desire to know eventually converges with that of my desire for meaning. We have already seen that the desire for meaning intends an intelligible, coherent, meaningful world. The myths of mankind and the stories of his religions have been born out of the spontaneous conviction that order prevails over chaos, that the absurd is not the final word, or that reality is intelligible. Now we must ask whether the statement "reality is intelligible" is also the postulate undergirding my desire to know. If it is not, then the two desires will forever remain in conflict.

Duality of Desiring

It is easy for me to recognize in myself an insatiable hunger for meaning and still refuse to accept as my own any belief scheme that seems designed to satisfy it. For another appetite intervenes, if I have given it liberty, and it seeks a more sobering sort of satisfaction that may subvert the former urge. The need to be honest, to face the facts squarely, may render any vision suspect that appeals to the craving for a God-centered story in which to embed my fragile existence. I can fully trust the instinct to be honest, to "face reality," whereas I must be wary of jumping headlong into the current leading toward affirmation of any transcendent source of meaning, especially one associated with the many meanings of the word "God."

In *The Myth of Sisyphus* Albert Camus gave vent to his own personal anguish at experiencing in himself two powerful but mutually antagonistic drives. On the one hand there was his desire for meaning, for unity, a "longing to solve," a "need for clarity and cohesion."[2] On the other hand persisted his desire to know. He expressed the priority of the latter in his rejection of any temptation to lie to himself about a possible transcendent meaning to the universe. His professed refusal to deceive himself led him to reject any "leaps" of faith or metaphysical flights that constructed worlds of transcendent meaning.[3] Camus, like Freud and countless others, illustrates how the desire to know the real can edge over any other desires in human consciousness if it is given liberty to do so.

We find time and again individuals who will entrust themselves totally to what they readily identify as their disinterested desire to know the truth. And on the basis of this commitment they will reject any vision that speaks to them of the ultimate intellibibility of the world. They will even confess to a passionate preference for a coherent universe. They would like a religious outlook to be the correct one. And they would be delighted if their desire to know were commensurate with the "will to believe." But their need to know the real "as it is" precludes such wishful thinking.

Colin Wilson in his book *The Outsider* provides numerous examples of individuals afflicted with this inner tension:

> This is the Outsider's extremity. He does not prefer *not to* believe; he doesn't like feeling that futility gets the last word in the universe; his human nature would like to find something it can answer to with complete assent. But his honesty prevents his accepting a solution he cannot reason about. His next question is naturally: Supposing a solution *does* exist somewhere, undreamed of by me, inconceivable to me, can I yet hope that *it might one day force itself upon me* without my committing myself to a preliminary gesture of faith which (in point of fact) I cannot make?[4]

As stated earlier, we would have to admit, with Camus, that we live in an absurd world if that desire in us which, with its imperatives, impels us toward the real did not ultimately support the desire for meaning. We have noted what happens when the merger of these two desires is forced prematurely: "meaning is gained but the self is lost." And we have also alluded to the possible consequences of altogether rejecting the feasibility of any such connection: persistent inability to participate in any story is a basis for experience of meaninglessness and in some cases psychic disturbance. This would indeed be an absurd world if, with Becker, we are forced inevitably to sacrifice epistemological integrity on the altar of psychic balance, if we always have to pursue meaning at the expense of honesty.

Critical reflection on the act of belief demands that we deliberately confront this question as to whether total commitment to the desire to know is really incompatible with meaningful belief in God. We must approach this problem in separate stages.

In the first part of what follows I shall argue that fidelity to one's desire to know, even when it leads through apparent meaninglessness, entails a discovery of hidden meaning which anticipates some form of narrative expression. And in the second part I shall argue on the basis of an analysis of its intentionality that the desire to know merges with the will to believe in God after all, for the dynamics of each is premised on the intention of an intelligible world.

There is an advantage to approaching the problem of knowledge and belief in this fashion. By an analysis of the intentionality of human desires we lay no claim to mastery of any specific content. We attempt no "proof" of God's "existence." And yet we can still confront the problem of knowledge and belief at its most vital nerve center: in the complex source of human desires that give rise both to "knowledge" and to the stories that provide the context for belief.

(1) Hidden Meaning

Meaning, I have said, is not experienced, lived, or felt adequately outside of some narrative framework. Without a story life will be experienced as absurd.

> The inability to tell a story leaves an unintelligible residue in our lives that is too large. There are too many feelings that lie fallow because we are not able to connect them with the reality of the self. The story can be viewed as an integrating structure that organizes our feelings and forms a sense of continuous identity. To live without a story is to be disconnected from our past and our future. Without a story we are bound to the immediacy of the moment, and we are forever losing our grip on the reality of our own identity with the passage of discrete moments.[5]

Sartre's Roquentin illustrates vividly the sense of alienation from story:

> I have never before had such a strong feeling that I was devoid of secret dimensions, confined within the limits of my body, from which airy thoughts float up like bubbles. I build memories with my present self. I am cast out, forsaken in the present: I vainly try to rejoin the past: I cannot escape.[6]
>
> I wanted the moments of my life to follow and order

themselves like those of a life remembered. You might as well try and catch time by the tail.[7]

This sense of meaninglessness is the result of a narrative breakdown. Such a breakdown can take place for any number of reasons. It may be that the story in which I am invited to participate is too challenging. Such a story might seek the allegiance of too much of myself. Or it may happen that the prevailing social or religious story does not seem capable of assimilating the many sides and energies of myself. In any case I am never wholly a participant nor totally nonparticipant. The meaning of my life is never firmly established except at the price of stagnation.

I am interested, however, especially in that kind of emptiness and meaninglessness that allegedly follows upon what is called "fidelity to experience," "facing reality," refusing to lie to oneself, or adherence to the imperatives to be attentive, intelligent and critical. Why should it happen, or need it happen that those who say they face the facts with severest honesty are often those who are most tormented with the problem of life's meaning? Is it never possible to discern the lineaments of some meaningful story capable of generating rather than veiling such relentless honesty?

I should like to argue that the courageous pursuit of honesty is itself modelled upon an archetypal story whose pattern provides the tissue from which a hidden meaning is apprehended without usually being theoretically formulated. And on the basis of such a disclosure I shall contend further that the intention of the desire to know is to strive toward an alliance with the narrative expression of the will to believe. In this manner I shall attempt to fashion a position that rejects the absurdist interpretation of the world and that affirms simultaneously the integrity of the acts of belief which affirm the ultimate intelligibility of the universe.

Sometimes their allegiance to the "reality principle" leads thinkers into stern resignation to the apparent indifference of the universe and from there to the explicit denial of any intrinsic cosmic meaning. Such stoicism arises out of "fidelity to experience" or commitment to intelligence. But this indefatigable loyalty to the demands of experience or reason reveals a courage that is made possible only by way of a silent sense of participation in some story beyond the fragmentary self. This is the story of the hero. The stoic or the absurdist is not initially aware of his putting on this story, just as most men are not explicitly alerted to the myths that provide their reality sense. But quite often the latent heroic tale eventually becomes explicit as in Camus's dredging up the myth of Sisyphus, Sartre's appeal to Orestes (refashioned, of course) or Nietzsche's myth of the Superman. Even from within the depths of emptiness and meaninglessness, I am inclined to think, there is often a veiled recognition of one's heroic confrontation with the monsters of our collective dreams. And the refusal to sacrifice one's desire to know by regressing through some primitive impulse to the inflated state of infantile (religious) bliss is a necessary phase in the heroic story. Having successfully endured the temptation to surrender his detached need for reality to the maternal urge for gratification or meaning, the hero then returns home to proclaim his new insight and yield over his treasure for others to share.

Such a journey may be explored through both mythical and ontological analysis. Joseph Campbell depicts the mythic adventure of the hero as involving the three phases of separation-initiation-return:

> A hero ventures forth from the world of common day into a region of supernatural wonder: fabulous forces are there encountered and a decisive victory is won: the hero comes back from this mysterious adventure with the power to bestow boons on his fellow-man.[8]

Even while engaged at a highly theoretical level in probing our blind and senseless universe, the absurdist participates in this narrative sequence at a primal level of world-involvement. Often elements from this dramatic undercurrent surface into his theory obviously enough to reveal the psychic bonds that prevent him from losing his balance in a pathological way. The absurdist may keep his sanity in an "absurd" world because he is still tied by a mythic life line to the common heroic adventures of mankind. It is only when he loses touch with the narrative sequence underlying his absurdist thought that he may eventually go insane. However per-

verse the stories of Sisyphus, Prometheus, Orestes or the Superman may appear to the religiously sensitive, the fact that these are
stories (and not abstract theories) is more significant than their actual content. Story-telling after all is a way of ordering the world.
And even when the world is said by theory to be intrinsically disor-
dered we still have to explain theoretically why, in the face of this
announcement, the impulse to tell or retell stories persists.

Story-telling may well fall among those recurrent human acts
that Peter Berger refers to as prototypical gestures.[9] These are impulses toward world-ordering that persist even while the intelligibility of the world is rejected in theory. Ordering, laughing,
hoping, and playing all at least *intend* a coherent universe even
though theory cannot always keep pace. I would add that narrative
consciousness also plays on the postulate that the absurd is not the
final word. And remarkably, it continues to function as the sub-
structure of those very theories that reject any permanent meaning
at the heart of things.

At a spontaneous level consciousness continues to function on
the premise that order prevails over chaos. Nothing less than this
could explain its persistence. This is most true of its resurgent tendency to shape the world with myth and story. Our prototypical
gestures seem to affirm repeatedly, and in spite of all obstacles,
that the absurd is not the final word, that it is not futile to search
for coherence in the universe. Ordering the world would not and
could not occur if there were a primal conviction that reality is absurd at heart. The spontaneous world-ordering acts of primal consciousness, especially those of story-telling, *postulate* a universe
which is essentially benign. Any other kind of universe would not
lay itself open to being ordered in any way. Because primal thinking has not yet made the theoretical distinction between the subject
and its world, it does not need to ask whether the universe *in itself*
is intelligibly ordered. Primal awareness is so intimately one with
its world that the order of consciousness is also the order of the totality, embracing what later become subject and object. Ordering
and looking upon the world as already ordered are one and the
same. They are different only to theory.

Do the lower, spontaneous reaches of consciousness, then,
have some privileged access to the real that places them far ahead

of theoretical consciousness? Or do we have to take the side of theory and renounce the fantasy-based projections of primal thinking?

It might occur to some that the impulse to tell stories is simply man's way of buffering himself against the void that he senses beneath all appearances but does not want to face head on. And the archetypal adventures of the hero are merely psychological necessities without metaphysical significance. The problem of ontology, however, cannot be so glibly suppressed. It is both legitimate and necessary to ask for that in virtue of which one continues to affirm himself as something (identifies with the hero) even after allegedly glimpsing his own nothingness. Whence is one empowered to create new meaning when he has wafted so deeply of meaninglessness?

It is in terms of this problem that we may introduce briefly the ontological considerations promised earlier. In this way we hope to point to the ground of narrative activity and its continuance even in the face of the absurdist's own theoretical denial of what such activity intends: a meaningful world. We may bring ontology into correspondence with narrative consciousness so that the prevailing dichotomy between the theoretical and primal patterns will be challenged at least in an embryonic way.

Such is the intent, I think, of Paul Tillich's ontological analysis of courage. In *The Courage to Be* Tillich asks how someone who experiences emptiness and meaninglessness may continue to accept and affirm himself in spite of this anxiety. For Tillich, as for the social scientists and philosophers discussed in Chapter IV, human vitality characteristically takes the form of intentionality.[10] That is to say, man's life differs from the animal's in that it is given to creating meaning rather than simply acting according to inalterable biological routines. Human life, therefore, receives its severest test when its push toward meaning is questioned or threatened. From an ontological point of view we must ask how a man can continue to *be* in the face of the threat of meaninglessness? Whence comes the courage to be, the power to affirm oneself, when what is most vital to human existence is threatened or apparently absent? Tillich responds that there is a hidden meaning in meaninglessness consisting of a participation in the power of being or Being-itself (God).[11] But I should like to add that this inarticulate sense of participation in the power of being is mediated symbolically through the persistent workings of narrative consciousness even when all stories are repudiated at the level of theory. As long as the narrative light flickers, however dimly, in the lower reaches of the self, the possibility of new meaning remains present. And this is enough to solidify a person's courage in the transition to a new way of relating to the world, or to a revised reality sense.

What Tillich calls the courage to be points to the ontological element in which narrative consciousness is ultimately rooted. Participation in the power of being is the source of our vigorous proclivity for ordering the world through stories. All of our prototypical gestures, moreover, postulate the ascendancy of meaning over meaninglessness, of being over nonbeing, of an intelligible universe over an indifferent one. Tillich's ontology simply expresses at the level of theory what consciousness postulates in the narrative mode.

This postulation of an intelligible world, I may now add, is also made implicitly by the pure desire to know. And it is because of this that I am maintaining its eventual alliance with the will to believe which activates narrative consciousness. Since this is the central point to be made in the present chapter I am obliged to expand on it considerably. My argument essentially is that the pure desire to know can itself be theoretically accounted for in all of its manifestations only if it is understood as converging with and supporting the will to believe. Such an argument can be provided only through a careful analysis of the prereflective intentionality of the pure desire to know.

(2) The Desire to Know and the Affirmation of God

That our universe is coherent, rational, or, as we shall say, "intelligible" and not absurd cannot be demonstrated scientifically. In fact, science goes a long way toward uncovering apparently blind and irrational elements in the emergent cosmos. Philosophy too has encountered countless objections in its attempts to prove that the world is rational or rooted in a hidden rational power. These attempted proofs with their corresponding objections are too numerous to detail here. But we should note that the naturalistic and philosophical quests for God have to a large extent been undertaken in the spirit of looking for an object. That is, they have uncritically followed the theoretic pattern that splits the world into object and subject, and from within such a configuration "God" can appear to the knower only as one object among other objects. Such a pursuit of the divine, then, is destined to fail, for all it is capable of uncovering are finite elements within the theoretically constituted world. Any hypothetical absolute that by definition transcends both subject and object cannot possibly be "found" by subject/object thinking.

Reacting vehemently against this objectifying quest for God by theory, many modern philosophers and theologians have insisted that God can only be apprehended from within the interpersonal field of meaning.[12] The reality of God can be affirmed exclusively in second-person language and not in the impersonal third-person discourse of theory. God is always essentially Thou. And any attempts to verify "Him" will inevitably be frustrated. Encounter, not verification by philosophy or science, is the only possible way of knowing the divine or, more strictly, of being known by the divine Subject.

From this point of view, however, it becomes questionable whether the philosopher can say anything positive about God at all. Philosophically theoretical analysis is seen as a distraction from the path of encounter with the Thou who is always Subject and never an object for thought. Arguments for God's existence are judged to be groping, and often misguided, questions rather than sources of evidence for God. Evidence for God is found only in revelatory dialogue with Him.

The problem with this reaction is that it remains unintelligible to the countless thoughtful men who put a high price on the theoretical approach. To someone immersed in theory it is not enough to ask him to substitute the interpersonal pattern. This will inevitably appear reactionary.

Going beyond theory, however, need not be regressive. In the previous chapter I attempted to show how talk about God can be modeled on language about "intelligent subjectivity" (and that God-talk may no more be ruled out a priori as meaningless than may talk about the self). Such an approach also involves going beyond the realm of theory but not in such a way as to renounce it. I have stressed the necessity of intellectual conversion for moving beyond a horizon determined strictly by common sense and theory. But the "turn to interiority" is not the same as substituting the primal for the theoretic mode of consciousness. The intellectual conversion of which I spoke expands one's horizon so as to embrace simultaneously the worlds opened up by primal consciousness, common sense, theory and subjectivity. It is not an exercise in regression to purely primal thinking. In the course of this book I have repeatedly invited the reader to open up his field of knowledge and reflection so as to allow it to include his own desire to know which is the basic element in his intelligent subjectivity. The case for God's reality, therefore, may be argued not simply in a primal, interpersonal, pretheoretical way but also in a "post-theoretical" way on the basis of one's awareness of his own desire to know. I would agree with the personalists that philosophy will be frustrated if it attempts to locate God within the horizon of theory alone. But I would not rule out philosophy's ability to make a case for a rational universe, grounded in a transempirical intelligence, on the basis of an expanded post-theoretical horizon. We must remember, however, that the problem in such argumentation does not consist in the formal reasoning involved so much as in the personal realization of horizon-expansion through the difficult process of conversion.

Duméry's caution applies to the argument that follows:

One must be ready to challenge all that one has, all that one is, all being, in order to discover the single incontestable that depends only upon itself and whose only foundation is its spontaneity: the Absolute, the One, God. This attitude is so daring that at this point it threatens all objective security, it severely upsets established habits that hesitate to adopt it or even to consider it correct. Of course it is impossible to make it known to those who do not "realize" it themselves; that would be the same as showing colors to a blind man. The defense of its validity becomes easier when objectivism and its logical techniques admit their insufficiency.[13]

In order to transcend objectivism, though, the subject must undergo the intellectual conversion described in the preceding chapter. Thus our argument in the following pages can make sense to the reader only on the condition that he now stands in a new horizon constituted by his own personal rejection of the idolatry of objectivism.

The existence of an ordered universe and the reality of a God in which it is grounded have always been two aspects of the same question. For, according to traditional arguments, if our universe is ordered in spite of all apparent evidence to the contrary, then (1) either this order is itself the result of an intelligent ordering, or (2) whatever order is evident in the universe is sheer happenstance. If the second option is the correct one then the universe in which we live could be called absurd after all, meaning without ultimate intelligibility or explanation. If the first option is correct, and this universe has a basic ordering principle, then we may call it a coherent one and therefore a universe open to the interpretation we have called belief. But the manner in which such determination has been made in the past has involved endless arguments about the objective evidence for order in the world. In the eighteenth and early nineteenth centuries, for example, Newtonian science made the world appear obviously "the work of an Almighty hand" (Addison). This world of marvelous mechanical regularity could be nothing less than the content of a divine design. But since Darwin such a benign picture of the world has often given way to one in which chance, millennial groping, waste and tragedy lurk behind the extravagantly complex veneer. And throughout history there have been isolated thinkers who asserted the priority of chaos over cosmos. Is this world pervasively ordered, we ask again today, or is not its order (especially in the complexification of organisms) an evanescent and local backward fluctuation in an essentially indifferent, entropic movement of matter?

Thus the argument for God from the order in the universe has encountered severe difficulties. Any argument appealing to "empirical evidence" for such design will be countered by others providing evidence of disorder and evil. Moreover, the objection has been made that such an argument still operates within the subject/object scheme and will inevitably fail to placate those who seek a truly transcendent Subject.

Any answer to the question whether the world is ordered or not requires clarification of what is meant by order. The meaning of order, as an intelligible arrangement of some sort or other, is dependent upon the type of questions we are prone to ask in seeking to understand phenomena. The world-to-be-known will vary according to the several methods employed by scientists or philosophers; thus its potential intelligibility may be grasped in different and complementary ways by different methods.[14] *Classical method*, that employed by Newton and Galileo, apprehends the world-to-be-known in the patterns of regularity, mathematically conceived, which pertain in a world reduced to primary qualities. But such a method leaves a residue of empirical data that remain unexplained by the abstractions of mechanism. So in order to take the patterns of the world more fully into account scientists have evolved what is called *statistical method*. The intelligibility grasped by this method is that in which probability of recurrence within schemes made up of large numbers of individual elements constitutes the world-to-be-known. But taken independently, classical and statistical methods do not seem capable of fully taking the "order" of the world into account. There is also the phenomenon of "emergence" in natural and cultural evolution that cannot be grasped until method becomes genetic. *Genetic method* apprehends the world-to-be-known as one in which development or shifts in the type of regularity grasped by classical and statistical method is taken into account in our anticipation and questioning. Such a world-order allows for what from the point of view of classical method alone would be unintelligible (such as the elements of randomness and groping in evolution). Finally, in order to account for the fact that many stages of natural and historical process are not directly intelligible, a *dialectical method* becomes necessary. Such a method allows us to tolerate momentary absence of intelligibility because it anticipates (without specifying) eventual resolution of apparent absurdity. Or, as the case may be, it notes where natural or cultural syntheses have broken back down into declining trends.

I have given this brief summary listing Lonergan's differentiation of four methods (classical, statistical, genetic and dialectic) in order to emphasize how complex is the question of the world's order and intelligibility. Often, especially in the philosophy of religion, it has been tacitly assumed that only classical method can determine whether the world is ordered, and therefore whether it contains evidence of a transcendent intelligent ground. Because of their fixation on classical method, arguments for God's existence on the basis of design in the universe have often been criticized in the wake of more recent revisions of method and awareness of the insufficiency of Newtonian science to account for all that occurs in our world. The scandal of randomness and apparent absurdity, which are taken into account by other methods, may thus give rise to two opposing interpretations by those who hold only to classical method. Either such deviations in world process are "direction which thou canst not see," i.e., elements of experience which further application of classical method could in principle account for, or else they are evidence that the world is not intelligible after all (since only if it conformed to classical schemes of recurrence could it be called intelligible). Over this question "theists" and "atheists" have often been polarized in a theoretical way.

The desire to know, however, as it moves in the field of theory, cannot entrust its attentiveness and questioning to only one of several prevalent methods if it is concerned with thorough understanding of the real. Thus it generates continual revisions of method commensurate with its passion for intelligibility. Whether the world is intelligible or not, therefore, cannot be decided on the basis of whether it fits classical method alone. For the world-to-be-known discloses varying styles of intelligibility corresponding to the various modes of anticipation inherent in all four methods (or any others that may appear in the future, should such occur).

Instead of arguing from "objective" evidence of order in the universe (corresponding to any particular method) I propose that our starting point be simply the *question* whether reality is intelligible. For the question whether reality is intelligible can, I think, be answered without having to appeal to direct and exhaustive evidence from the empirical sciences. The sciences in any case could not possibly have surveyed enough data to warrant any definitive hypothesis or judgment a posteriori. But if the universe of reality is intelligible, and if such intelligibility can be firmly established on some other basis than the sheer accumulation of external data, then we would have the main elements of an argument supporting theoretically the spontaneous claims of the believer.

I must repeat here that in order to understand what follows it is essential that one first have grasped and undergone what we have referred to in the previous chapter as intellectual conversion. Moreover, even intellectual conversion has links to narrative openness so that our argument may make sense only to one whose horizon allows it to do so primally as well as theoretically.

We begin then with the question: Is the universe, the whole of reality, absurd or intelligible? We would like to build a response, not by the frustrating search for concrete objective clues in the world of nature and man, but by an analysis of the conditions that make it possible for us even to ask the question we have just asked. How is it possible for me, the writer, and you, the reader, to ask whether our world is absurd or intelligible? Perhaps this question itself sounds peculiar, but it is a type of interrogation that has a fruitful and respected lineage in modern philosophy. It arises from a discontent with the naive questions that ask merely about the world of objects. Instead it stems from an interest in what makes it possible for us to ask questions at all, about anything. It seeks what Kant called transcendental knowledge as distinct from empirical knowledge.[15]

The desire to know that we have observed flowing through the various patterns of consciousness now, at length, turns back on itself from within the theoretic field in our attempt to understand why and how its imperatives and questions come streaming forth spontaneously. Without our having reflectively and deliberately established a program for so doing, we find ourselves already engaged in the world in a questioning and critical way. In the face of this irrefutable fact we may either say "so what" and continue to live at the unreflective level, or we may give in to imperatives inviting us to ask what makes it possible for us to be so engaged. What are the conditions in reality that make it possible for us to seek spontaneously after intelligibility in the world?

We shall argue that the basic condition necessary to call forth our questioning is that *reality is intelligible*. The apparent circularity is intended. Simultaneously with questioning, we spontaneously posit that there is intelligibility to be grasped in the world. Otherwise we would not have sought it out. There would be no questioning without the anticipation or foreknowledge, however hazy, of some answer. And we would not continually revise our methods did we not anticipate some further intelligibility. The hidden premise upon which the pure desire to know undertakes its audacious excursion in questioning is that the real is intelligible. When we ask whether reality is intelligible we have already posited such intelligibility as the horizon of our questioning. The only problem is whether we can both theoretically and personally accept and defend what we have, through our questioning foreknowledge, insisted upon. Is our questioning too presumptuous in its "foreknowledge" of intelligibility in the world? And when we ask whether the whole of reality is intelligible how can we say that such a question arises only because we have already somehow anticipated such intelligibility? Such are the central questions for our argument.

To recapitulate: either the universe is (1) fully intelligible and has some ultimate explanation, or else (2) it is an accident and therefore, as a whole, without intelligibility. These are the only possible options. Only one and at least one can satisfy my intelligence. If either of them is incapable in principle of explaining the dynamics of my pure desire to know then by definition it does not conform to reality (since we have understood reality to be the objective of this desire). If, on the other hand, one of the alternatives does correspond structurally to my desire to know reality then I can accept it intelligently and critically without having to amass exhaustive data from the observable world in order to establish my point.

The only one of the two options that is compatible with what I can confirm about my desire to know is the one that affirms the intelligibility of reality as a whole. But the argument can have no impact unless the reader reflects in a deeply personal way on his own desire to know. He must himself ask which of the two visions of reality provides the conditions which allow *him* to ask questions, to seek intelligibility and to make judgments. The argument, if it is convincing, will flow forth from the reader's own intimate self-awareness, and this itself is the largest part of the problem. The most the writer can do is make suggestions as to what steps such self-reflection might take. Ultimately the impact of this argument is contingent upon the degree of self-appropriation a person has achieved. Remembering what we have said in the previous chapter concerning the necessity of conversion in self-knowledge, our "argument" is inevitably of a different nature from those that take place simply in terms of formal logic and natural science. It is essentially intended to reach conclusions that can only result from each person's own internal dialogue with himself and his desires. And such a dialogue involves more than keenness of intellect.

We have set forth in this book a series of steps that the reader might use as a guide to stimulate his own progression toward cognitional self-understanding. But whether such self-understanding requires the vision that the world is intelligible and not absurd demands a judgment which will not follow automatically but only out of the depths of each person's own life. We should not altogether exclude elements of risk and courage from such a possible judgment. For a great deal more is at stake here than we would have in a simple deduction of formal logic.

The Basis of the Argument: Implicit Trust in the Desire to Know

Recall what was established already in Chapter I concerning the pure desire to know, its imperatives and its objective, reality. Recall also that we have understood reality as the objective of the pure desire to know. Illusion we have defined as the imagined projection of fulfillment of some other desire than the pure desire to know. The objective of the desire to know is the intelligible, the real and the good: The imperative "be intelligent" leads us toward apprehending the intelligible; the imperative "be critical" drives us toward affirmation of the real; and the imperative "be responsible" impels us toward the good. When understood as the objective of the pure desire to know therefore, the intelligible, the real and the good are convertible notions. The real *is* the intelligible and the good. Our world therefore cannot be held to be absurd and unintelligible if we have any faith at all in our desire to know. For to hold that one cannot trust his desire to know, or to hold that one's intelligence leads inevitably to spurious results is itself a judgment which can arise only from implicit and spontaneous faith in one's powers of intelligence and criticism. We have already submitted respectfully to the mind's imperatives at the same moment in which we doubt their worth. Our performative appeal to the integrity of our thinking and judging always refutes any explicit suspicion of their value.

The inadequacy of the absurdist position is not demonstrable by bringing up concrete instances of order and goodness in the universe. Rather its inadequacy can be grasped only through a process of self-reflection whereby one suddenly grasps the disproportion between what he has said about reality ("reality is absurd") and the trust he has given to his own powers to grasp intelligibility and make critical judgments. In short the absurdist interpretation of the world is ruled out if and when a person can say out of his own depths: "I am a knower." This self-affirmation, however, is not easily or automatically achieved. The argument of this book has been that this self-knowledge is realized most readily in a religiously narrative context.

An Inevitable Objection

Undoubtedly readers will be bewildered by the claims that I have made. Many will agree with Milton K. Munitz; to say that the universe

> . . . as the "wider domain to which the observed universe belongs," is literally a complete, unique, and intelligibly structured whole, is a claim to which we need not commit ourselves. It should be left open as an unresolvable question, for it is something on which, properly speaking, we do not have any knowledge. To stipulate that it *is* so, by definition, is of course, no way of establishing this knowledge.[16]

Are we not still merely wishfully thinking and not really knowing when we posit with the believer the intelligibility of the whole? And when we advert to the sometimes overwhelming fact of absurdity and to the countless apparently unintelligible events in our experience does not our argument simply suffer from inattentiveness? After all, one of our mind's imperatives prods us to be attentive and open to all the data of experience. Have we heeded this precept at all?

Munitz would argue that we may not have done so.

> For the world may contain elements of disorder, or refractory indeterminateness, that would frustrate any drive to all-encompassing intelligibility. If there were such elements of "chaos" or indeterminateness in the world, they would never be known or understood, since to know them would imply they are intelligible, and so would be contradictory of our assumption.[17]

In response to this I can only paraphrase Lonergan. Outside of being there is nothing. But being (or reality) has been defined as the objective of the pure desire to know. Therefore nothing lies outside of this objective.[18] Consequently Munitz's hypothesized elements of chaos, falling outside of the intelligible, would not be part of reality but would rather be "nothing." We have not maintained, however, that "nothing" is the objective of the pure desire to know.

Now Professor Munitz might object to our calling being the "objective of the pure desire to know." Perhaps, he might conjecture, there are ontic, unintelligible *facts* that lie outside of the scope of this desire. Perhaps reality is not in every aspect intelligible. He seems to be saying that we shall never know whether or not this is the case.

However, I would say that for something to be any type of *fact* at all, it must be capable of being somehow experienced, intelligently grasped and reasonably affirmed. It must lie open to attentiveness, intelligence and judgment. Therefore, it must be at least intelligible before it can be affirmed as fact. It is nonsense to talk about a possible *fact* which is intrinsically unintelligible, for one must *grasp* before he verifies something as factual. Thus, if

Munitz's hypothesized universe (involving elements that are inherently unintelligible) is the one existing in fact, then the *factual* existence of such a universe would have to be open to the grasp of intelligence and the affirmation of judgment. But Munitz insists quite rightly that it is impossible in principle to make such a judgment in the case of his projected universe. If, then, no judgment of fact is possible in principle concerning the existence of a universe involving elements of inherent unintelligibility, then Munitz's imagined universe is also unintelligible and his talking about it is meaningless. I would have to follow Lonergan's conclusion, then, that the real world (the one existing in *fact*) must be an intelligible one, one capable of being completely understood.

This does not mean, however, that the *data* of my experience in this world are already understood or ever will be by human beings. Indeed nothing in my experience appears to be fully understood. Questions for understanding continue to arise the more I attend to the data of my experience. And this is why I can become continually more aware that the universe is a baffling mystery to me the more I attend to it. By technologically enhancing the sensory apparatus whereby I see the microscopic world beneath and the galactic world above, questions for understanding come streaming forth ever more prolifically. However, the awareness of complex new questions arising from enriched experience can become so dizzying at times that a curious extrapolation is made: from the obvious fact that *I* have not fully understood my limited experience of the universe I am tempted to jump to the contention that the universe is in itself not fully intelligible.

Such an inference is often made, I am afraid, in the service of some other desire than the pure desire to know. My desire to know urges me to be attentive. but the more closely I attend, the more questions arise, displaying my ignorance of the universe. As I strive to understand, the more the field expands to which I have to attend. And the more this occurs the more questions continue to arise. The chasm yawns ever wider between my actual understanding and the yet-to-be-understood universe opening up before me in my questions. My way of shrinking from this abyss may be to deny that the universe is fully intelligible. For if it is fully intelligible, and my own actual understanding has advanced no further than this, then the extent of my knowledge shows up as so vanishingly minute that I cannot accept the conception of myself implied herein. The shortest flight from the awareness of my nothingness is to project onto the universe the very poverty from which I myself suffer. Thus I would be tempted to say that, perhaps, the universe is not so intelligible after all. In making such a statement, however, I may be finally capitulating to the will to mastery after following my desire to know up to a point of crisis.

I would like to be as faithful as possible to the imperative to be attentive. And I am not oblivious to the experiences that continually compel us to ask how the world can be intelligible if people die and children suffer, if earthquakes and famines occur, and if groping, chance, and waste are involved in the evolution of life. I would not want to close my eyes to any of these facts or to the problems our minds have making sense of the universe. But, as I have shown in the previous chapter, the scope of attentiveness (and of the questions for intelligence that arise from attending) is determined by the dimensions of my horizon. And I attempted to show there that through the experience of intellectual conversion the horizon opening up to the data to be attended to and made into material for understanding now includes my desire to know. I must also heed the imperatives to be attentive to, to be intelligent and critical about that desire which urges me to be attentive, intelligent and critical. This is what I am attempting in this chapter.

Because of what I consider to be an expanded horizon I think I can be even more attentive to the full range of data of my experience than can the philosopher who wants to stick to no other givens than those of sense experience or to the data of scientific work. I seek to understand why I am driven to be attentive, intelligent, critical (and responsible) at all. I want to leave no datum unquestioned, including my desire to know. It is remarkable that we all experience, however dimly, a desire to know, but how little we attend to it or try to understand it! I am arguing that the more we attend to it, the more questions will arise as to how to understand and explain it. And I am maintaining that the only explanation of it which is coherent to me is the one which holds that I would have no desire to know were not reality intelligible as a whole in spite of its obvious elements of chaos and evil.

However, every hypothesis or explanation seeks verification. We cannot be content with mere thinking. Being attentive and intelligent is not enough. We must also be critical. How do we critically verify that explanation which holds that our desire to know seeks intelligibility, reality, and the good only because reality *is* indeed as a whole intelligible and good? Since a posteriori experimentation is ruled out, what other mode of verification is possible? Here again we must recognize that the content of our questioning is determined by the breadth of our horizon. To those for whom all explanations must receive verification by empirical method the results of any other verification procedure would be meaningless (since meaning also is a function of horizon). Thus, as I have repeatedly stated, the argument will indeed be meaningless to anyone who has not experienced intellectual conversion with its reconstitution of horizon. To one who has experienced this conversion, however, the verification of our argument occurs simultaneously with his appropriation of himself as a knower. Only one who has accomplished this to any degree will understand what I mean and thus be in a position to verify the argument.

Furthermore, I have argued (especially in Chapter III) that such open willingness to follow the desire to know as it leads through successive conversions and rebuilding of horizons may itself require an attitude that can only take root in a consciousness resonant with religious symbols. Openness, understood as the grateful acceptance of this desire to know and its primacy over other desires, can hardly exist in the realm of theory if it is not also present in the sentient, interpersonal, narrative and aesthetic modes. But the way in which one's character achieves openness at the primal level is typically through religious conversion with its essential element of gratitude.

In Chapter III we understood as normatively religious those symbols and stories motivating us first at a primal level to grateful acceptance of our creatureliness. This is not the sole function of religious symbols. But the acceptance of finitude to which they motivate the religious is necessary for humble acceptance of the radical openness of the desire to know. For the latter's unrestrictedness always by contrast shows up the poverty of our actual attainments of knowledge. In the face of this shock the courage to accept finitude is required. Unless we remain aware of the openness of our desire to know we will easily allow the will to power or omniscience to suffuse the fields of meaning, including the theoretic. Consequently an appropriation of religiously symbolic language by primal consciousness may be a necessary *de facto* condition for undergoing the horizon shifts required for apprehending the meaningfulness of God-talk in a post-theoretical way.[19] The validation of God-talk, therefore, first requires conversion to that horizon in which such talk would at least be meaningful. But conversion is not an automatic operation of the mind. It is a radical personal shift of horizon demanding risk of self and, above all, openness of character. And, finally, this openness of character may need to be brought about by what we have called "religious conversion."

Therefore, the theoretical (or better, post-theoretical) "argument" for the reality of God, can occur meaningfully only on soil prepared by an openness in the primal fields of intentionality. More specifically, there must already be some participation in the type of self-revising story that promotes openness of character if the horizon shift prerequisite to any theoretically meaningful "argument" for God's reality is to be a possibility. Theorizing about the existence of God is probably vacuous outside of any prior narrative involvement in religious stories and symbols with their sentient, interpersonal and aesthetic overtones.

Why, then, has there been so much interest in the question whether God's existence can be proven, especially if any meaningful validation requires a prior narrative-religious self-involvement? I think there may be several different motives behind such interest, corresponding to the desires that we have discussed. Interest in proofs for God's existence may arise from motives as far apart as, on the one hand, the disinterested desire to know and on the other, the obsession with certitude that is one instance of the will to mastery. The attempt to verify God's existence theoretically may stem either from an attitude of openness or from a refusal to accept the native openness inherent in the desire to know.

The need to avoid wishful thinking or accusations of illusory projection of primitive desire will often lead those believers whose consciousness moves in the theoretic field to establish a case for

God's existence from within this field. They do so in order to heed the mind's critical imperative. They have, of course, already accepted the congruity, value and validity of belief in a primal way. They now want to do so theoretically. Such believers remain aware that their "knowledge" of God is not considerably expanded by moving into the theoretic pattern. For religious knowledge of God is essentially symbolic and therefore sentient, interpersonal, etc. But recognizing how easily human desires of all sorts may inhabit the primal fields, the theory-influenced believer may want further to test the validity of his belief by subjecting it to some sort of verificational process in which detachment from such desires appears more explicit. Such a process, however, is clearly ambiguous because of the subject/object approach to which theory is consigned. For this reason, I have advocated that the theoretically oriented should use in their quest for God a validation process modeled on the search for and understanding of human subjectivity. Otherwise they may become embroiled in the futile and religiously unacceptable search for a divine "object."

It is in the attempt to verify God as an "object" of theoretical knowledge that the obsession with certitude may be the dominant motivating impulse. It is entirely possible that a highly "rational" approach by the theologian or philosopher may mask an unwillingness to participate in religious-symbolic existence at the primal level. The theologian too is subject to being more strongly influenced by the drive to mastery than by the desire to know. Theology is distinct from religion in that it reflects upon religious life from within the theoretic pattern. Such reflection becomes necessary whenever the consciousness of the believer embraces the theoretic mode. But there is always the danger that the theologian will be seduced into forcing religious consciousness too rigorously into this objectifying pattern. And in so doing he may be disparaging the primal types of knowledge that are essential to the religious, including the theologian himself. Theoretical knowledge is not a substitute for the sentient, interpersonal, narrative and aesthetic cognition of the sacred apprehended in the symbols of primal awareness. The theologian, too, is susceptible to that form of idolatry which fetishizes the theoretic mode and thus leaves human life impoverished.

Perhaps what I have written in this chapter is disappointing to those whose explicit interest in the world is dominantly theoretical and objectivist. But my intention has been to show how and in what instances belief is compatible with and flows out of the pure desire to know, not how it may be tailored to correspond to theory, and, within theory, to classical method. For I sense in such attempts at accommodation a motivation inconsistent with the pure desire that does not confine itself exclusively to any one pattern of experience or any one method of cognition.

Conclusion

In anticipating the complete intelligibility of the world the desire to know takes sides with the intentions of the will to believe. It is not so keyed on the theoretic pattern that it is incapable of also respecting the cognitional worth of the narrative mode. Being, or reality, is not grasped apart from a "reality sense." And the latter is the product of the story in which we participate.

The pure, detached desire to know being does not and cannot require total disengagement from the narrative mode of awareness. It does, however, strive to liberate itself from story-fixations. Story-fixations occur whenever the will to meaning splits off from the pure desire to know, thus allowing other desires, especially the will to mastery, to energize the narrative field. When this happens, one's reality sense becomes frozen and inflexible. And if "religion" and "God-talk" are associated with such a rigidified reality sense they draw the justifiable critique of those who sense that the desire to know has been stultified by divine sanction.

Both the desire for meaning and the desire to know strive toward unity. But the nature of this unity is different in each case. The unity grasped at by the will to meaning is liable to be provisional and partial. But the oneness toward which the desire to know tends is comprehensive and absolute. It is because the basic drive moves relentlessly toward a more remote and all-inclusive unity that it refuses to tolerate for long the narrative schemes of meaning that we devise to provide momentary relief from our restlessness. The desire to know is capable of condoning diversity, fragmentation and even meaninglessness not because it accepts these as ultimate, but because it seeks an ever-wider and richer unity and intelligibility. Karl Jaspers writes:

> The realization of diversity is not indifference to unity . . . but a will to true unity. In any such premature unity as we are often seductively offered, truth itself is not attained. Disjunction, because it is an unbearable experience, keeps us in search of a unity that no question can shake. We want the one true unity, since nothing else will give us peace.[20]

The desire to know is not, as Camus thinks, opposed to the desire for meaning. But it constantly shatters the specific contents of our stories lest we deem them absolute. The two desires are in constant tension, but as the will to meaning opens itself to the desire to know, the goals of the two drives converge. And in the end the will to meaning will find the promise for its realization to lie in a full commitment to the desire to know.

As a consequence of these considerations we must recognize that not every story, and not every use of religious symbolism and God-language has been faithful to the requirements of the desire to know. Not every use of religion promotes self-acceptance as we have understood it. In the following chapter, therefore, we shall set forth certain criteria that will have to be fulfilled in our story-telling and story-participation if we are not to do violence to our basic drive. That is, we must ask how stories of God motivate persons to a self-acceptance radical enough to put them in touch with their desire to know and all of its demands.

VII
Religious Story and
Self-Acceptance

Perhaps the area in which detachment from self-interest and bias is most difficult to achieve is that of self-knowledge. Acceptance of myself *as I really am* is the most frustrating assignment given to my desire to know. The testimony of the world's religion, philosophy and literature on this matter is too obvious to require detailed support. How can I secure the detachment required by my desire to know as it strives toward the goal of self-knowledge and self-acceptance?

The obstacles to self-acceptance and the reasons for failure of self-knowledge are numerous. Prominent among theories of self-deception provided today are those that stem directly from Freud or Sartre. And there are many other theories that fuse existentialist with psychoanalytic explanations. A convenient synthesis of some of these is provided by Herbert Fingarette in his book entitled *Self-Deception*. Like Kierkegaard, Freud, Sartre and many others, Fingarette is baffled by the fact that the desire to know can so easily be suppressed with respect to the very self out of which it emanates:

Were a portrait of man to be drawn, one in which there would be highlighted whatever is most human, be it noble or ignoble, we should surely place well in the foreground man's enormous capacity for self-deception. The task of representing this most intimate, secret gesture would not be much easier were we to turn to what philosophers have said. Philosophical attempts to elucidate the concept of self-deception have ended in paradox —or in loss from sight of the elusive phenomenon itself. . . .

143

What, then, shall we make of the self-deceiver, the one who is both the doer and the sufferer? Our fundamental categories are placed squarely at odds with one another.[1]

The phenomenon of self-deception is perhaps always intimately connected with the awareness of guilt. Some sense of guilt appears to be a pervasive human phenomenon. And in a world influenced by biblical religion with its heightening of the ethical dimension of human existence, awareness of moral inadequacy is at times intense beyond endurance. Augustine and Luther stand out as paradigmatic instances of the self-torment to which moral introspection can lead those who have awakened to their responsibility. Their writings testify to the difficulty they both had in coming to self-knowledge. Sensing the gap between possibilities and actual moral achievements can lead to despair. And if one is not capable of handling the anxiety of guilt, that is, if one cannot accept himself in spite of guilt, then various forms of self-deceit, often pathological, may take hold of consciousness. Such deceit remains a paradox to the philosopher. The refusal to accept oneself, fully to know and face one's "dark" side, is the most puzzling instance we have yet encountered of repression of the desire to know.

According to Fingarette the self-deceiver is one who refuses to avow that he is engaged in the world in a particular way. Using our own categories we may say that self-deception is the state in which a person narratively or theoretically understands himself in a manner out of joint with his sentient, interpersonal and aesthetic stance. He feels about himself or others in a way that is not "spelled out" in his self-story or in attempts to objectify himself in theoretical terms. Thus he invents a "cover story" in order to rationalize this state of internal disproportion, in order to fill in the gaps that always accompany this policy of self-distortion.

Self-deception, Fingarette insists, is possible only if there is already a certain amount of integrity of character.[2] I would not hide from myself did I not aspire to be morally or socially worthy. Such aspiration indicates that I do not totally identify with dark tendencies. The sociopath does not have such aspirations and so does not need to deceive himself. In fact, Fingarette thinks that the development of a capacity for self-deception is a sign of growth in the case of those who previously were immune to conflicts. Self-deception paradoxically implies a blossoming aspiration toward values and possibilities not previously assimilated by consciousness.[3] Still it remains opaque to philosophical theory. And the theoretician is not as such able to remove a state of self-deception in others or himself.

In whatever manner we state the problem of self-deception, acceptance of self requires most generally speaking a realignment of my self-understanding with the intention of my desire to know. But my contention throughout has been that the identification of myself with this longing cannot be accomplished in a purely theoretical way. I must also seek the narrative framework within which all of my primal sensibilities may be reattuned to the movements of my basic drive. Only in the framework of some story will I be able to embrace the awareness of guilt from which I flee and so be liberated to embrace my possibilities. The flight from guilt-awareness is motivated by my reluctance to face myself as having possibilities transcending my given condition. And these possibilities take root only in an imagination steeped in some narrative pattern of world-arrangement. What would such a narrative be like? We shall attempt to provide an example at the end of this chapter.

The paradox of self-deception may be partially clarified in terms of the distinctions I have drawn among the intentional fields. Simply stated, self-deception is the result of disproportion and mutual maladjustment among these fields of meaning. For instance, sentient consciousness might construe its "world" so as to conform to a mood of light-heartedness. There are times when such a mood is the appropriate response to reality, at a wedding for example. The atmosphere of a wedding cannot be appropriately apprehended aside from such a mood. And so we may safely say that such light-heartedness is in the service of the desire to know on such an occasion. But suppose (as sometimes happens) that this same sentient tone is carried over into the whole sweep of one's various engagements with his world. Perhaps the sheer sensual gratification of the mood leads one to project an interpersonal, narrative and aesthetic world in such a way as to fit this and only this mood. Finally one approaches himself with the same levity and struggles desperately against any feeling tones that would allow him to penetrate deeper levels of his character. The neurotic, for example, often finds only one mood to be "valid" and absolutizes it as the only way to read the "real" world. We may assume that such a person is deceiving himself. The other modes of awareness are not allowed to mediate the world in accord with their unique styles of intentionality. And so the essentially polyvalent consciousness of a person gets disproportionate and distorted respect in the sentient field.

Another common example of such ambiguous and partial accommodation of the desire to know oneself is provided by psychotherapists: A person has an emotional problem, depression or some form of guilt-anxiety. In seeking to dispel it he reads all the relevant psychotherapeutic literature. He is able to diagnose himself and even understand himself quite adequately as far as theory is concerned. He seeks thus to know himself "objectively." He is convinced that he fully understands himself and is no longer under the spell of self-deception. While in a limited sense this may be so at a theoretical level, he continues to remain engaged in the world through the primal modes with the same degree of sentient disturbance, interpersonal isolation, aesthetic distortion and most important of all, narrative emptiness. He knows his guilt theoretically, but without the participatory stance required for knowledge in the other modes his deceit of self persists.

In an illuminating article, Leslie Farber notes the limitation of this objectifying approach to oneself in psychoanalysis:

> . . . while run-away subjectivity interferes with analytic progress, and some "objective" perfection of one's self and one's feelings is essential, this requirement is seldom served by the rather unnaturally and irrelevantly detached self-scrutiny that absorption with theoretical formulae invites. Achieving some objectivity toward oneself and assigning scholarly and hyphenated labels to one's symptoms are far from identical operations; scientific objectivity is not, if you will excuse me, subjective objectivity; it is, in fact, its opposite and enemy when the two are confused.[4]

Even though therapists differ from one another in theory, their patients come to acceptance of themselves only through the intersubjective "therapeutic alliance"[5] and not by grasping psychoanalytic or any other type of theory. In fact, restriction of self to theory is an obstacle to the interpersonal insight provided by the alliance of patient and therapist in which purely objectifying thinking must be relativized. And the hypostatization of theory may interfere with the patient's underlying quest for a narrative context commensurate with his cognitive and emotive needs. The disproportionate weight accorded to objectifying introspection is just one more example of the absolutizing instinct that lies at the heart of the patient's problems in the first place.[6] Overcoming this absolutizing tendency requires an opening up of self-awareness through the narrative and other primal fields as well. The need for personal openness demands the search for a story in which decentralization of the ego may occur without the contrivance of theory.

Religious Myth and the Problem of Self-Deception

How is the paradox of self-deception possible? Why do we refuse to follow the desire to know ourselves? And how do we induce the state of self-acceptance in ourselves and others who have lost it?

Long before philosophical reflection or social science were faced with these issues, religious myths attempted to respond to them. Myths of evil narrate how people were led astray, seduced, blinded and, as a result, brought into evil. The myths tell how this event of evil is followed by a sense of self-rejection (exile, despair, blinding). But they then go on to relate how redemption from or within such a state is possible also. And in the telling and acting out of the myth, the participants gain a sense of renewal.

We need not describe these myths here, for they are well known.[7] We must emphasize once again, however, that the narrative mode that the myths employ has responded to human anxiety about evil in a way that no philosophical or theological theorizing can adequately compensate for in a "post-mythical" age. Moreover, these myths of the origin and end of evil have provided the contexts in which men have experienced the courage to face and accept the sense of defilement, guilt, sin, and human inadequacy in a way that theoretical reflection cannot achieve on its own. In motivating people to self-acceptance in spite of fate or guilt such myths can be seen as emanating from, rather than resisting, the pure desire to know. They have assisted rather than frustrated the drive for self-knowledge. The myths of evil and redemption provide the milieu in which people are able, even eager, to face their lives as they really are. Later I shall provide an illustration of how such a myth can function and how without such a mythical setting self-deception is perhaps inevitable. And I shall set forth the thesis that self-deception is all the more possible the more the fissure widens between the narrative and theoretic modes of world-intention, the more consciousness loses touch with the naive thinking of myths of evil and redemption.

Before doing so, however, I am obliged to take note of a most articulate objection to the thesis I am setting forth. It comes from Jean-Paul Sartre, and it holds that religious myth is itself a prime instance of "bad faith." By bad faith Sartre means the act of self-deception in which a person refuses to accept total responsibility for himself and his actions.[8] Bad faith is that act or state of rejecting the underlying awareness of radical freedom which is given with existence. Belief in God, for example, is an act of bad faith because it turns over to some Other this radical freedom. In fact, the very idea of God is itself the construct of bad faith. And all religious myths share in this self-deception.

For Sartre, therefore, acceptance of self involves the rejection of the God of bad faith. A critique of the notion of a Necessary Being into which we escape from our freedom is a necessary step in coming to realistic awareness of the nothingness that we are.

In the myths of evil there is an element that Sartre would find especially repugnant. The myths all postulate that evil is in some way anterior to man's free acts. In many archaic myths man comes onto the scene only after the forces of good and evil have already clashed and cosmos has virtually prevailed over chaos. The resurgence of chaos in nature and in human life is therefore not totally the responsibility of man. Evil is somehow already there. It is the result of fate, to which even the gods are subject. Or it is intrinsic to matter and carnality. Or else it is the environing chaos that is never totally dispelled by the redeemer. And even in the Adamic myth where human freedom is highlighted there is the Serpent who again symbolizes the anteriority of evil with respect to human willing and action.[9] Sartre's doctrine of radical human freedom cannot embrace these myths.[10] For they all seem to steal from man and attribute to some alien and mythic power a portion of the freedom to do evil that human reality possesses. Thus those who adhere to these myths put on masks that allow them to hide not only from others but also from themselves.

Once man is stripped of these myths he is allowed to face the fullness of his freedom, his own radical responsibility for "evil." Sartre thinks that authenticity, overcoming bad faith, requires an appropriation of the radical freedom from which man tries to escape in giving responsibility for evil to mythic powers antecedent to his own existence and acts. Full self-acceptance, therefore, demands the extirpation of one's life from any such narrative involvement.[11]

How, in the face of such notable opposition can I maintain that self-acceptance is possible only on the condition that I be involved in a narratively symbolic way with some "myth" of evil's origin and end? Does not my proposal lead toward, rather than away from, self-deception?

My answer to this is in two parts: First, Sartre would be correct and I would be deceiving myself if in fact man is free in the radical sense that Sartre defends. I shall not develop this point except to say that I do not think Sartre's doctrine of a radical human freedom based on man's nothingness could be coherently built up if he reflected adequately on his own desire to know. Prior to his arrival at the "fact" of his own nothingness (which is the necessary condition for *radical* human freedom) Sartre is carried along by his own desire to know. This desire is a spontaneously given inclination (not one methodically chosen from point zero) to determine what is the case with respect to "human reality." Sartre attends to his own existence, gets an insight into it, conceptualizes and expresses it in his plays and philosophical essays. And in response to the imperatives "be reflective" and "be critical" he affirms: "It is the case that man is nothingness." Now in his own performative use of this "*is*" Sartre refutes in act what he affirms in his theory.

For anyone to be able to judge that something *is* the case, there has to be an implicit obeisance to the demands of the real, of being. In any *judgment* there is a comparison of what one thinks ("man is essentially nothingness") with ontological criteria not of his own making. It is the implicit appeal to these independent criteria that makes his judgment acceptable to another. If man were radically self-creative, as Sartre contends, if man created himself out of his own nothingness, this would entail that his insights and judgments (such as "man is nothingness") also emanate from his nothingness. But how can Sartre hope to convince either himself or his readers that it is really (*in fact*) the case that "man is nothingness" unless he implicitly accepts the priority of independent criteria of being over his own consciousness? His performative use of the verb "to be" in his judgment is evidence that human consciousness is always already dependent on being for its critical activity. This is what makes it possible for one person to share his knowledge with another. Man is not pure nothingness but rather a being striving for more being. This is most evident in the distinctions he makes between judgment and mere thinking. It is in aligning himself with his deepest striving that his freedom consists, a striving that is not his own creation but which motivates him to create himself, to transcend himself. It is in accepting his own desire to know that he avoids self-deception or bad faith. Whatever assists him in this task, a sense of humor or a religious myth, cannot be as such a manifestation of self-evasion.

The second part of my response to Sartre's critique of religious myths may be more to the point. I think that Sartre's own attempts to overcome bad faith have a narrative underside, something akin to a myth of evil, without which the personal acceptance of his own "nothingness" is impossible. Neither Sartre nor anyone else can experience the courage of self-acceptance without a primal participation in narrative symbols of deliverance from defilement. Theorizing alone is insufficient. In this sense Sartre's myth shares the basic features of the religious myths of evil.

All myths of evil posit a duality between the *actual* state of guilt, suffering, evil, etc., and the *essential* condition from which the actual is a deviation, and toward which the acts of redemption narrated by the myth are directed. Sartre's thought shares with myth this duality between the actual and the essential. The actual, defiled condition is that of being in bad faith. The *essential* condition is that of self-knowledge. Sartre's writings, both theoretical and dramatic, tell the story of the redemptive transition from the actual to the essential. As in the myths of evil the essential (deliverance from bad faith) is never actually achieved in an adequate way, but the aspiration and tension between the actual and essential is no less pronounced. In reading Sartre I do not theoretically advert to this narrative undercurrent, at least at first. The appeal that he has to me in his condemnation of self-deception[12] is one that is *felt* at levels of my world-involvement which are not merely theoretical. I feel challenged, even shaken. I cannot remain theoretically detached. His writings (much more than those of a logical positivist, for example) solicit the attention of all the primal fields of meaning. Sartre appeals to people not just because he is a genius as a philosophical theoretician, but because his writings enliven the whole range of intentional structures, including the one in which myth-making occurs. Sartre's own recognition of this fact leads him to use the novel and the play to convey his insights. The courage to be that Tillich exalts in cases of Sartrean self-acceptance is not without a lively narrative infrastructure. And in a most unobtrusive way this dynamic foundation anticipates a "redeemed" state of affairs that energizes sentient, interpersonal and aesthetic existence requisite for human vitality. It is only when one gives up at the primal level as well as the theoretical that pathological and suicidal forms of despair take over. Sartre in any case is not without a rather lively story of his own, one that has undergone repeated revisions in the course of his lifetime.

In this sense I do not consider Sartre's thought to be an obstacle to our quest for a narrative pattern that motivates humans toward ongoing attitudes of self-acceptance. Moreover, his own expressed concern for authenticity has roots in the very story that I shall use later to illustrate my point.

The most arduous terrain over which the pure desire to know struggles for liberation is that of self-knowledge. And without self-knowledge the awareness of others and of reality in general may also suffer. Self-acceptance is the condition of knowledge in the primal sphere of engagement. Thus if we can make a case for the necessity of some religiously narrative involvement in the act of self-acceptance, then we may say in a general way that stories of God may originate in the need to know and not exclusively in the flight from reality or self.

Religion and Cover-Stories

Recent psychotherapy has given ample support to the conviction that awareness of guilt is often if not always ingredient to self-deception.[13] The flight from insight into self would not occur did I not already somehow know that my actual condition is painfully distant from an ideal toward which I aspire but which I also seek to evade. Restoration of insight requires, therefore, a "spelling out" of this dim and repressed awareness of myself.

> In general, the person in self-deception is a person of whom it is a patent characteristic that even when normally appropriate he *persistently* avoids spelling-out some feature of his engagement in the world. . . . This inability to spell-out is not a lack of skill or strength; it is the adherence to a policy (tacitly) adopted.[14]

> A self-covering policy of this kind tends to generate a more or less elaborate "cover-story." For a natural consequence is the protective attempt on the part of the person to use elements of the skill he has developed in spelling-out as inventively as possible in order to fill in plausibly the gaps created by his self-covering policy. He will try to do this in a way which renders the "story" as internally consistent and natural as possible, and as closely conforming as possible to the evident facts. Out of this protective tactic emerge the masks, disguises, rationalizations and superficialities of self-deception in all its forms.[15]

I must link my self-understanding to some narrative structure, even when this understanding is insincere. I thus generate my own story to fit not my desire to know but some other desire, such as the urge to conform to an overly idealized image of myself. In any case, no matter what policy I follow, flowing from whatever desire,

I spontaneously seek some narrative representation of this policy. Sincerity with respect to myself, therefore, also requires spelling out through a story in which is imprinted the dynamic self-revising intentions of a disinterested yet passionate desire to know myself.

I do not know of any story, religious or otherwise, that unequivocally bears this imprint. For the same narrative framework that originally exhibits detached concern for the real may always be utilized by impulses of a self-serving nature. I shall advance the proposal, however, that the only image or story of God that can fully satisfy the requirements of the basic drive is one which narrates His unconditional acceptance of man. And my reason for hypothesizing in this way is, as I shall try to clarify in this chapter, the necessity of self-acceptance as the condition for appropriate release of the dynamic urge to know.

Self-acceptance is the prerequisite for genuine and animating adherence to the imperatives of the mind. I cannot be fully open to the world, to others, to beauty without being open to myself. Whatever inspires openness to myself, therefore, must somehow flow out of an underlying desire to know. Images of God that present Him as cruel, law-oriented, severe, repressive (of which religious history abounds) can serve only to hide me from myself. Such images originate projectively out of inclinations toward power and mastery, and they support the armor of cover-stories that prevent us from penetrating deeper into ourselves. They are objectionable not only on psychotherapeutic but also on epistemological grounds. If an image or story of God presents Him as repressive in any way then the philosopher along with the theologian and therapist is obliged to reject such an image as illusory (i.e., as flowing from some other desire than the pure desire to know). In order to allow for the liberation of the full depth of human desire, one's image of God must eventually be refined away from any paternalistic, coercive, perhaps even "theistic" qualities. To affirm the reality of God with the fullness of oneself must be functionally equivalent to acceptance of all of one's desires and inclinations without embarrassment.[16]

Why, it may be asked, would anyone be inclined to adhere to a demonic image of God? Why, indeed, has the repressive deity always been a possibility and consequently evoked so much "atheistic" repulsion? Such grotesque accounts of God, we might safely say, originate in the flight from insight. They appear in direct proportion to the absence of self-acceptance by "religious" people. What is theory permitted to say about such images of God that always originate independently of any theory? And on what basis can the philosopher make his judgments? The remainder of this chapter will attempt a response to these questions.

A Critique of God-Images

The goal of philosophy is self-appropriation. Anything less than this would render it sterile, empty and uninteresting. It is a quest for those factors that would facilitate my acceptance *as my own* of the imperatives which are always operative in my questioning and knowing. In short, its goal is freedom. Theory is not able all by itself to bring about a fully personal "yes" to my underlying restlessness of spirit, but it is able to point to those elements of human life that can mediate the freedom and courage of self-acceptance. It is within its ambit, therefore, to inquire into the function of God-images or stories of God in the process of coming to self-acceptance.

It is impossible adequately to evaluate a God-image independently of the feelings it evokes in the lives of particular people. The image of God may call forth a wide variety of sentient response. For example, the image of the Creator may either summon forth feelings of gratitude or it may provoke the sense of hamstrung freedom and power to affirm life. Much depends upon the stage of development an individual has reached. A child will project or transfer onto the image of God associations that would be abandoned by an adult. And in general the cultural and psychological determinants of the image of God will vary considerably from one person to another. Thus the feelings aroused by the God-image will be correspondingly diverse and complex. In some cases the image will be able to conjure up feelings of self-acceptance. But in others it may contribute to self-deception, and if, as often happens, it has degenerated into a demonic image, it may even precipitate a state of self-rejection.

Consequently, we are not permitted to make any definitive

statement about the function or truth-value of an image or story of God without simultaneously taking into consideration the peculiar quality of the feeling-response evoked by the image in any particular individual. All we may say in this matter is that the feeling of self-acceptance is the indispensable foundation for a deeply personal appropriation of the mind's imperatives. And whenever the image of God is a factor in promoting sentient consciousness toward this attitude of self-appreciation it may not be casually disregarded by the philosopher whose primary interest also is the subject's coming to grips with himself. It is within the ambit of a philosophy of religion to ask about the way in which an image of God may block or promote the feeling of self-acceptance.

There is a sense in which the problem of God is not so much whether God exists as *what* is God. The question "*Quid Deus sit*" is a prologue to the question "*An Deus sit.*" We have held that the question of validity is systematically prior to the question of the meaning or value of discourse about God. But psychologically and chronologically the question of validity arises only subsequently to the question what God is like. Unless a God-image first evokes some primal concern or wholesome feeling the question of its veracity will not meaningfully arise, nor should it arise. Only if God-talk stimulates the feeling of self-respect and respect for others would we be interested in its truth-value. For this reason it is easy to understand why modern critics of God-talk disclaim its validity whenever they notice its failure to promote concern for self and others.

On the other hand philosophers of religion often overlook the truth-value of the primal religious feeling of self-acceptance when it does occur. There is a way in which it is possible for the philosopher to give approval to religious narrative whenever involvement in stories of God is the occasion for self-acceptance, for honesty and for satisfaction of man's basic drive. The feeling of self-acceptance is indispensable for the promotion of the dynamic desire to know toward its unrestricted objective. It cannot, therefore, be dismissed in these cases as merely fanciful feeling. Yet there are serious questions as to whether and how a God-image can motivate a sense of honesty with respect to oneself. We shall now proceed to treat some of these.

The "Atheistic" Moment in Self-Acceptance

Acceptance of the deepest layers of one's desiring is a process, a movement, a becoming that never reaches a final point of rest. To describe such a process, then, is always to abstract from and freeze artificially what is essentially fluid and quietless. Thus our reflections in this chapter are severely limited and are in no sense a substitute for the actual process of immersion of oneself ever more fully in the stream of desiring. Nevertheless, I think we can make some useful observations about certain landmarks that might be recognizable as we pierce deeper levels of our restlessness. I am referring in this discussion of landmarks to the transmutation of God-image that occurs as the process toward self-knowledge evolves. These may offer at least vague criteria as to the degree of self-acceptance one has reached. Obviously the significance of our discussion will be felt more completely by those who have related at one time or another to some image or images of God than to those who have not.

We have held that our fundamental eros is the desire to know the real. And we have noted that the degree of participation in and acceptance of this drive is measured by the intensity of our fidelity to the imperatives that flow spontaneously out of this desire. What we have not yet sufficiently adverted to is the varying degrees of proximity to the center of interest that the inescapable imperatives of our basic drive may have at various points in our life. Modern psychology has helped us to see how, especially when we are young, we tend to project these imperatives onto others so that initially we experience them extrinsically or heteronomously. We are not yet aware of the inner origin of the precepts and so, to a great extent (though never totally), we experience our young lives as shaped by external factors. Our sensitivity and patterns of intelligence are socially molded. Our critical capacities are not yet developed, and our sense of responsibility, in particular, is originally not fully our own, but predominantly introjected into consciousness through the social institutions in which we are nurtured. Consequently the basic drive and its imperatives do not initially appear to occupy a central place in self-consciousness. And throughout life there remains at least a residue of the child's appeal to others to think, reflect and decide for him.

As growth occurs, however, the direction of nature's development seems to urge us toward a continually more intimate and explicit association of the center of the self with the mind's imperatives. This growth generally brings with it both a sense of self-esteem and an increasing anxiety in the face of the developing experience of autonomy. If one is not capable of appropriating the loneliness of his emergent freedom he will experience the temptation to regress to a heteronomous state of existence once more. Thus defense mechanisms arise through which an individual pretends to escape from the stirrings toward autonomous integrity of thought and action that the precepts of the mind require.

In order to prevent the imperatives from appearing as though they spring from the inmost depths of oneself the individual may, among other defenses, cling desperately to the heteronomous image of God that is the religious correlate of the child's extrinsicist experience of the norms of his mind. This God then becomes the screen on which he projects his desire to be governed from outside. And the image of God that was normal and healthy in childhood—for the child the God-image inevitably and rightly involves elements of heteronomy—is held on to by the adult as a way of resisting the natural pressure toward self-appropriation.

Even when it means the repression of normal feelings of growing autonomy that would come from an acceptance of the imperatives *as my own*, I might still find it more congenial to live in the clear-cut "safe" world of extraneous, projected norms. Then I never feel these norms as flowing from the "I want," but only from what someone else wants.

Eventually, though, there may come a point when the pressure toward autonomous assimilation of the imperatives of the mind impels one to rebellion against the "God" who has prevented him from "being himself." This is what we may call the "atheistic" moment in growth toward self-acceptance. At times it occurs so smoothly as not to be noticed. But at other times it happens dramatically, and it may be accompanied by bitterness toward "religion" in general and against the church in particular. Then, because religions and churches are not themselves exempt from legitimate accusation for promoting infantile notions of God in many instances, the newly liberated "adult" may persist in putting all the blame on them for his own failure to grow. In this way, however, he still manifests an inability to accept himself fully as critical and responsible since his blaming is just the inverse way of saying "I wanted you to judge and decide for me, but you let me down."

So the atheistic moment is ambiguous. And the blaming and bitterness that often accompany it are infallible signs that the goal of self-acceptance lies a long way down the road.

Because freedom is a difficult gift to accept, we are always ready to surrender it. There is a never fully conquered urge to return to the world of magic, manipulation and heteronomy. We never fully coincide with our basic drive, never quite tune our spirit to its own restlessness. Thus we may find that the imagination for a time oscillates back and forth between the magical world of the child on the one hand and, on the other, the apparently indifferent, empty universe that appears when the magician-God is dethroned.

But then there may occur another phase in which one still feels compelled to wonder in gratitude at the freedom that dawns when he begins to associate himself ever more closely with the imperatives that have always been present to his consciousness but from which he has hidden in a variety of ways. At this juncture for the believer the "God above God"[17] may transfigure the archaic images of childhood. The God above God appears when one is able to give thanks for his freedom, when he accepts the imperatives of his mind not as a restraint but as a gift. This is an aspect of what the theologian refers to as the experience of grace.

What is meant by this curious designation, the "God above God"? According to Tillich it is only when the total otherness of God is transcended and one finds himself "beyond the God of theism," only when God is experienced as transpersonal, as the "ground of personality"[18] rather than totally subsumed by personalistic categories that I can begin to sense the depths of my own personal freedom. As long as God appears only as the "other" over against me, watching me, approving or condemning me, my freedom will remain buried. My judgments, decisions and actions will not be experienced as flowing from deep within; they will be carried out at a distance from the center of myself and so will not really be mine. I will always have an eye out for what the authority in heaven wants of me. And so I may continue to remain out of touch with what *I* want, refusing to admit it, even to myself, as long as the divine guide hovers over me. This form of self-deception may be the most difficult kind to overcome because it is fortified by the fear that rebellion against the severe paternalistic God would be the ultimate act of self-annihilation. (Whereas in fact it may symbolize the beginning of a very healthy process of decentralization of an *ego* obsessed with its own perfection.) And so a person will remain on the level of intellectual and moral infantilism, justifying his psychic immobility by appeal to "God." This pathetic but common state of mind is characterized by the hidden premise that what I want most deeply simply cannot spontaneously correspond with the "will of God." Therefore, I must continually sacrifice my natural wanting to what He wants. And when I do find myself occasionally following my spontaneous leanings I may be riddled by feelings of guilt analogous to those that Freud associated with the Oedipus complex.

Our approach in this book has been to show that one need not fear associating himself with his natural desires. And our reason for this confidence lies in the conviction that the kernel of human desiring is the reproachless desire to know. If at bottom our longing were perverse, then we might have cause to deny it. But in acknowledging the natural inclination toward the good, the true, toward freedom and love we have every reason to embrace our desiring in its totality. In order to reach the basic layer of striving it is inevitable that we will have to make our way through other, ambiguous desires. But repression would always be self-defeating. It will happen, of course, that as we identify with the "I want" which is with us from infancy we will become entangled in desires that may not lead us directly to accept as our own the imperatives of our minds. But until we take the risk of fully admitting to ourselves that we do have many wants and needs, we will not take the first step toward aligning ourselves with the fundamental desire whose promise is freedom. I shall argue that in order to do so we must look for a "story" that provides the context in which we can freely avow all of our inclinations.

The mind's imperatives must be experienced as intimately my

own if they are ever to lead to unaffected freedom of thought and action. But in order to gain this freedom I must cease experiencing them as though they are imposed on me from some Source totally outside of myself, standing over me and using me as a vessel into which He pours precepts that never really seem to emerge from myself. In the quest for freedom the notion of a personal God is quite ambiguous, for if I project onto God only anthropomorphically "personal" features, especially paternalistic ones, without also adverting to the transpersonal elements that religious experience also attributes to the sacred, I may easily allow God to become the demonic outsider, the source of my alienation from my desire, never allowing me to coincide with myself. This is not to say that God must no longer be addressed as Thou. Some mode of dialogue is essential to the believer. What it does demand, however, is that God must also be experienced as the depth of my own subjectivity and not exclusively as a Subject situated opposite me. Only in this mode of religious experience could I experience the imperatives as simultaneously my own and still rooted in a principle transcending me in some way, guaranteeing that my autonomy not degenerate into self-idolatry.

Henry Duméry, like Tillich and a number of other philosophers of religion, insists upon the necessity of going beyond "the Absolute of dialogue" as a condition for experiencing one's freedom.

> It is well known how much the religious consciousness seems attached to an Absolute of dialogue. By criticizing the latter do we not irremediably compromise the religious exchange between God and man? No; the most that can be said is that criticism withdraws this exchange from psychological and sociological metaphors in order to situate it on a more profound plane. The dialogue no longer goes from the *ego* to the divine *alter ego* (that representation would be a distortion). It goes from spiritual singularity to God's productive simplicity which creates the spirit as self-creator.[19]

Some such development, I would agree, is essential for one's appropriation of the mind's imperatives. Otherwise there will remain a residual projecting onto an alien font of norms what is really an internal exigency. This may happen even if God is conceived of solely as a beneficent intervener:

> A God who is merely a benefactor will remain always paternalistic; this is an improvement over a tyrant but it is still a subtle alienation. Only a God who is capable of granting a share in his spontaneity can assure the salvation and dignity of the spirit.[20]

The believer must not be afraid to assimilate as a moment in his religious development the "atheistic" experience of someone like Nietzsche or Sartre. Some appreciation of their feelings and thoughts about God may be required to arrive at the point of accepting the roots of the believer's own freedom or to achieve the perspective from which he can give thanks for his autonomy rather than being resentful that God's beneficence is not "objectively" obvious. The believer must even carry his faith beyond the anthropomorphic oscillations of the God of justice and mercy, constantly witnessing from outside man's thoughts and actions.

> Psychological piety readily takes God as a conscience-witness. . . . The God-witness is like a double of the personal conscience; it is its judge (this provokes fear) and also its refuge (this evokes confidence and abandon). The God of justice thus becomes, and without inconsistency, the God of mercy. However, if this ambivalence is not transcended, the absolute, according to the criticism of Nietzsche (and some contemporaries), remains a God of weakness who distributes the premiums of security and offers celestial eternity as an alibi for terrestrial engagement.[21]

Standing with the atheist in the voidful silence of a universe stripped of magic and coercion is a necessary step in the believer's withdrawal of his projection onto God "out there" of the precepts that emanate from the depths of his own subjectivity. And if he is to continue affirming the reality of the Absolute, the affirmation must now be accompanied by gratitude for the void in which alone the self can fearlessly appropriate the promptings that up until now have seemed extrinsic and adventitious.

I will repeat here what I insisted upon earlier. Unless this new experience of selfhood is suffused with an atmosphere of gratefulness (although it may not always be clear to whom or to what this attitude is addressed) the possibility will re-emerge that one will hand over his freedom again, not to the God of childhood projection but to one or more of the primitive drives of which we have spoken: a will to power, obsession with certitude, etc. "Then the last stage of the man will be worse than the first."

What sustains the "religious" quality of the development we have treated in this section is the act of thanksgiving. The experience of autonomy in self-appropriation is not something one can be indifferent about. It will either precipitate a movement toward emptiness, despair and perhaps self-idolatry or it will evoke a renewed sense of gratitude. If the latter occurs, however, a problem arises as to how to express this feeling religiously. One finds that the prevalent religious exercises still employ the mythic and anthropomorphic imagery with which the immature associations of God were previously bound up. How can one still be a believer in God now that he experiences the mind's imperatives as his own, now that he is becoming aware of his freedom? Is there any continuity between the God of childhood and the Absolute of the adult? Or is the adult who affirms the reality of God condemned to a heteronomous existence and destined thereby to a life of bad faith, never to be fully in touch with his basic drive?

In answer to this we may say that it is not merely speculative theology or philosophy of religion but also the spontaneous religious life of mankind which points the way toward the transcendence of theism. It provides for the transitions of which we are speaking here, even though theology does not always recognize them. The fixations of theism occur when a theology, philosophy or spirituality excise one moment of the religious mode of understanding and idolatrously establish it as normatively religious. Unfortunately this has occurred in a great deal of Western theology and spirituality. Thus when the distaste for such idolatry develops to a sufficient degree it is expressed in so-called nihilistic or atheistic modes of thought and action.

From the point of view of the emerging broader perspective on man's religious life, however, such atheism may at times be viewed as an essentially religious phenomenon, elucidating an aspect of the experience of God that theism and its corresponding spirituality are incapable of reaching or understanding. This is what may be called the apophatic or kenotic side of God, God's silence and self-abandonment.[22]

When one's image of God comprises this moment of God's self-emptying withdrawal from the finite world then the creature and the world may be experienced as standing up in autonomous self-identity. They are no longer threatened or manipulated by an overwhelming and nihilating Presence. The religious response to this withdrawal or self-absenting of the Absolute is perhaps most appropriately that of silence. The apprehension of the burning absence of God leaves one most appropriately speechless. To fill the void with words may be to defile it. The experience of "nothingness" is an extremely important aspect of religious experience, and our obsessive Occidental verbalizing has caused us to overlook it. "The problem of God does not lie in the realm of theory. It does not belong to the realm of the word, but to the kingdom of silence."[23]

It is this aspect of religious experience that needs to be recaptured if the believer is to feel fully the identity of himself with his desire to know and to act out of his own initiative. The silence of God is implied in the refusal of Yahweh to give his name to Moses, in the image of the crucified God, in the silence of Buddhism and in the many religious symbols of divine kenosis. Systematic theology and philosophy have not satisfactorily brought forth this apophatic aspect of religious experience. But it seems essential now that they do so if they have any concern for the believer's quest for self-identity and maturity of thought and action. They must recognize that much so-called atheism has outrun them, albeit ambiguously, in reaffirming the silence of God within which alone the autonomy of the individual can come into view. In a religious consciousness attuned to the silence of the Absolute the world is thus allowed to be itself. And each individual may then freely and unrestrainedly delve into the depths of his own desiring. When the coercive deity of "theism" is transcended in religious development there is no longer any apprehension that what one really, deeply desires can come into conflict with some *extrinsic* Source of norms for thought and action. When such a threat is overcome one may, without guilt or repression, allow the buried layers of his striving to make their way to the surface. As the fundamental levels begin to erupt, they may, of course, stir up the various and cumulative strata of other repressed inclinations. Thus it is to be expected that the initial phase in the liberation of repressed human longing may involve the deliberate violation of sexual taboos and moral prescriptions of various kinds. And it may even happen that a sudden lifting of repression may allow the release of aggressive and destructive drives that seek vengeance on any "authoritative" figure or institution.

We must not overlook the potentially tragic and demonic results of the precipitous release of human desire brought about by the transcendence of theism. But we must simultaneously recognize the possibility that in this transition there is also the potential for a liberating appropriation of oneself as an attentive, intelligent, critical and responsible subject—provided that the development does not get stuck again in the "atheistic" phase wherein the required response of gratitude for the new experience of autonomy may be suppressed.

Those who go beyond theism often call themselves atheists. Such a label, however, is vague and misleading for in itself it says nothing about the intensity of a person's commitment to the imperatives of his mind. But in those cases where the "atheist" renounces theism in the name of fidelity to his own desire to know we have a phenomenon that from the point of view of an "apophatic" religion or theology may be called itself a "religious" development.

Such atheism is often a reaction against the idolatrous theism that attempts to freeze God in the position of a heteronomous agent of manipulation and magic. In his movement away from theism, therefore, the atheist understandably wants to abandon all talk about God as alienating and meaningless. He prefers to stand in the chaotic impersonality of a universe emancipated from "providential" control. From within this silence he begins to feel more deeply than ever before (what the theist may not feel) the welling up of desires that are intimately his own. He is no longer fearful of owning them. He may initiate a process of self-acceptance that the premises of a heteronomous theism never would have allowed. He finds himself alone and he senses a certain terror in this fact. But the newly acquired sense of coinciding with himself makes the sacrifice of his former state of being passively lived by others and their desires well worth the price. He may experience a sense of being estranged but it is at least not alienation from himself. He senses previously untapped energy rising in his consciousness and in his whole organism. At this point he may be able to say intensely for the first time, "I am." And, at the same time, he will be able to accept himself more fully as a questioner and knower. He will insist that it is his "atheism" which has made this new growth in self-awareness possible.

Does not this experience, testified to by many thoughtful individuals, contradict the thesis we have presented in this book, that continuing self-appropriation requires a narrative involvement in religious symbolism? Only if by "religious" we mean the heteronomous condition of projecting onto the heavens the paternalistic image of a God-authority whose essential function is to moderate human thought and action. It is no exaggeration to say that this is a prevalent way of imaging the Absolute. But at the end of our reflections we must emphatically reject it as subversive of the process of self-appropriation. Is there any other God, or story of God, many will ask? And the fact that such a question does arise so often is a betrayal of the deplorable state of religious education in our Jewish and Christian history. There is a still prevalent lack of awareness of the requirements of the human psyche with respect to the God-image at various stages along life's way. But there is just as little awareness of the way in which the religious experience of mankind has itself often spontaneously, dynamically gone beyond images of deity that the average Western believer assumes to be normative, eternally established, incapable of modification. More faithful attention to the data of religious life would show, I think, that the exigencies of the human psyche and human striving have often been satisfied by the involuntary dialectic in religious life itself.[24] But theologians and teachers of the tradition have often apotheosized specific phases of the evolution of the God-image without being alert to the whole pattern of its unfolding. And this has been to the detriment of human growth and self-acceptance.

From the point of view of our own starting point, that philosophy's essential concern is self-appropriation, we may issue some critical remarks about the way in which the religious story of God as Creator and Redeemer has often been accepted. And we shall also offer some suggestions as to how it must be read if the believer is to arrive at a depth experience of himself as a knower. Further, we shall propose once more that an ongoing attempt to avoid self-deception and bad faith may profit considerably from participation in a mature reading of the biblical drama. We shall review the story of St. Paul's conversion in order to exemplify this proposal.

Creation and Redemption

The story of God as Creator and Redeemer is often the object of "atheistic" rebuke because the symbols of creation and redemption both seem at times to require the response of passivity and helplessness that we associate with the state of heteronomy. "If gods existed, what could man create?" (Nietzsche) And if the image of God as Creator provokes a sense of impotence, so also may the story of redemption. The Christian tradition on this subject may be read in a variety of ways, one of which is expressed by Sam Keen, a man who has been quite sensitive to the relationship between religion, theology and human growth:

I have a growing conviction that the Christian presence in Western civilization has perpetuated a disease in order to offer a cure. It has encouraged schizophrenia by insisting that man is a sinner (estranged from self, others, nature, and God) who can do nothing to save himself. Indeed, all attempts at self-help are indications of pride which only deepen sin. The word "Pelagian" has been used to anathematize those who believe human freedom is potent. . . . The hard core of Christian tradition has always insisted upon the impotence and bondage of the human will. It has said loud and clear—"You can't. You can't heal yourself. Your only hope is in accepting *the* physician sent from God" (whose credentials are certified by the church).

This we know about psychopathology—at the heart of "illness" is the impotent child who is still crying, "I can't. You do it for me." And it is clear that the moment in therapy when the patient begins to "get well" is when he says, "I am responsible for my feelings, my actions and my style of life. In spite of parents, family, friends or the surrounding culture, I alone can make the decision to outgrow my dis-ease and to establish a way of life that is satisfying. There is no magic. There is no automatic dispenser of grace. There are no saviors. My final dignity is in my ability to choose my style of life."[25]

Keen's sentiments represent what I also would consider to be for many believers an essential stage, but only a stage, in the movement toward self-appropriation. The reading of Christian soteriology presented here is manifestly controversial. One does not have to abandon for the sake of self-appropriation the story that God is giver and man receiver. The story may be revised without being forsaken. This is how criticism operates in the narrative mode. The concept and feeling of what is given alters, in the process of human growth, but the element of wonder and gratitude must be a constant. Initially one wants magic. And when his prayers are answered by the providential magician he is grateful. When they are not he is filled with resentfulness. This is the heteronomous style of life that we may never totally outgrow. Eventually, though, one may reach the point in life where he can spontaneously give thanks that the world is not magical, but instead mysterious. He may begin to understand that if the world is seen as magically subject to divine manipulation human subjects would be also buffeted and restrained by the coerciveness of the universe. There could be no free subjectivity in such a world. But when the magical world disappears and after the initial phase of resentment has passed, gratitude may then flood the soul in a manner never anticipated by the helpless. Then the Good News is: "You are free and you will find yourself becoming graceful as you assume the responsibility for yourself and others."[26] Then a profound meaning of the story of creation is felt. Now one has his own autonomy to give thanks for. And redemption no longer means being acted upon magically from without by an extraneous and alien physician. Redemption now implies an experiencing of what we are calling autonomy (Tillich's "theonomy"). It connotes a participation in the freedom which dawns when the magical world-view is transcended and the silence of the Self-withdrawing Absolute invites the fullness and depth of human desiring to express itself.

An Example

How may the story of creation and redemption concretely undergo this transition from a heteronomous reading to one in which a person's freedom is awakened and accepted? How may we illustrate such a narrative revision?

Philosophical reflection on religious life must evaluate religious stories in the context of their use by particular persons at particular times. A general case can hardly be made for or against the truth of stories of God apart from the careful scrutinizing of the biographies and autobiographies of individuals. A religious story can properly be evaluated only as it intersects with concrete human lives. If a philosopher of religion attempts to abstract a religious story from its context in a particular consciousness and freeze it theoretically he will not be able to say much about it. After all, the philosopher is concerned with how a religious narrative relates to the imperatives of the mind. But he cannot ascertain this without attending to concrete instances of religious involvement. And he should be aware that the same narrative symbols that for one person enhance the sense of wonder, may for another close the world off to consciousness. There is a sense in which it cannot be denied that religion is what each person does with his solitariness.[27] Religion does not exist in abstraction from particular persons. It should not be evaluated as though it were.

The great religions of the world have always blossomed forth from or around some notable personage whose life inspires attitudes of self-accepting freedom in the devotees. It is to this remarkable ability on the part of religious persons to arouse these feelings of self-acceptance that we must look to understand the relation of religion to the desire to know.

As an instance of this narrative power to dispel self-deception and to inspire the courage of self-knowledge let us look at St. Paul's appropriation of the story of Jesus of Nazareth. His struggle to accept Jesus' own encounter with God is simultaneously Paul's struggle to accept himself. A clearer example of the intimacy of the two themes of faith and self-acceptance is hard to find.

Before his conversion, the story that shaped the identity of Saul of Tarsus was the one in which righteousness or personal fulfillment consisted in adherence to the Jewish Law as interpreted by Gamaliel and the Pharisaic tradition. The Law laid out the parameters of his life, bound together its multiple episodes and thus gave meaning to Saul's existence. So completely was his identity given by this narrative framework that upon his conversion Saul's name was changed to Paul. Such reappellation followed the general Semitic tendency to associate identity with name and to assign a new one on the occasion of undergoing a dramatic shift of horizon.

Saul of Tarsus related his life to the Jewish story in such a way that while he found meaning in it, layers of his personality must have remained buried and untapped by the traditional setting. As his conversion testifies, elements of his desiring and striving were not fully satiated by the Pharisaic rendition of the Hebrew story.

Both the psychologist and the philosopher may attempt to isolate and clarify the nature of the desiring that could not be accommodated fully by this "cover-story." We know that any desire may be the dominant one in a conversion experience. But the only conversion experience that could be acceptable on the basis of epistemological and psychological criteria is one which flows out of the openness of the drive to know. Many so-called "conversions" are acts of "regressive restoration" carried out in the service of the need for certitude, the need for security, or to escape responsibility; anything but the need to grow or the need for freedom. Only a conversion that awakens sensitivity, enhances insight and intensifies critical reflection could be acceptable on the basis of criteria that we have employed in this book and which, I have said, are inherently beyond reproach. The psychologist and philosopher are called upon quite legitimately by the religious to assist them in the task of sorting out underlying motives for conversion. And the way to carry out such an audacious experiment both philosophically and psychologically is to try to determine the degree of self-acceptance manifested in the convert, the degree to which he has emerged from bad faith and self-deception. Although this is a difficult task, it is not impossible. We find ourselves doing it all the time spontaneously. We should not eschew systematic attempts to discern genuineness of character either.

Is it possible to ascertain what the motivating drives were in the case of the conversion of St. Paul? The only leads we have by which to make such an assessment are, of course, Paul's writings to early Christian Churches. It is impossible for us to objectify Paul's inner experience, but it is possible to study how he expressed it in his life and letters.

Prior to his conversion, according to his own testimony, Paul thought that he knew himself well and that he was exercising his responsibilities in accordance with sound judgment. After his conversion he looks back at his former ways of thinking and acting and he sees his life as a lie, as a futile pursuit of self-justification measured by the heteronomous prescriptions that structured his world. One of the basic changes wrought by his conversion was his ability to avow thoughts and actions as self-deceptive that he formerly had envisioned as righteous. His persecution of Christians originally undertaken in apparently absolute conviction of integrity is subsequently confessed as sinful. What has occurred in this conversion?

The decisive element in his self-transformation from heteronomy to a new feeling of freedom was apparently a sudden and dramatic shift in the image and story of God. The transition to a new sense of God as the Father of Jesus allowed him to confess and avow his previous self-deception and bad faith, something he was unable to do from within the context of his previous religious certitudes. In other words a narrative revision, a new turn in his quest for meaning, a revised story of God as Creator and Redeemer was necessary for Paul's new insight into himself.

What was the essence of this narrative revision? Briefly and directly stated, the God of Jesus' story was suddenly seen by Paul as a God of unconditional acceptance, a God who accepts man in spite of evil and inadequacy, irrespective of man's attempts to achieve salvation by works. The significance of such a God-image cannot be grasped adequately except in terms of the problem of self-deception. Why do we deceive ourselves? Obviously because we are subject to being dominated by other desires than a pure desire to know. Why this should be possible is a subject that only religious myths of evil, and not theory, seem to be able to deal with. And there is no way in which these myths can be fully translated into theoretical accounts telling objectively why it is possible for blindness and evil to occur in that being who is essentially reality oriented. Philosophy is compelled to return again and again to the mythic confessions that recount in symbolic, dramatic form the origin of the estrangement which we have formulated as the disproportion among our desires. At this point reflection is confronted with mystery and irresolvable paradox. For some philosophers this impasse is the source of a frustration which inspires continued theoretical denials of any incomprehensible or ineffable liberating element in the real world. For others it is at this point that philosophy has shown its true colors, namely, in bringing consciousness back to the primal spheres and their openness to mystery out of which reflection emerged in the first place.

I too would judge philosophical reflection to be successful to the extent that it returns our consciousness in a new (post-critical) way to the sense of openness and wonder which only primal, narrative consciousness can inspire. The destiny of theoretical reflection is to return again and again to the myths out of which it was born in order to draw from the inexhaustible richness that they hold and in order to prevent its own collapse into sterility and empty speculation.

In a way that cannot be theoretically formulated, the story of the God of unconditional accepting love was able so to enliven Paul's striving that he was enabled to look more deeply into himself than ever before. His previous self-deception sprang from his efforts toward self-justification and from an inability to coincide with his own spontaneous striving. If he could but live up to the ideals projected by the Law then, he must have thought, he would be saved. However, if Paul's self-deception was structurally analogous to that portrayed by Fingarette, then he must have been engaged in the world (as in his persecution of Christians and in his fanatical fervor toward the Jewish Law) in a manner out of joint with some deeper sensitivities. There were clearly aspects in his own theological training that may have intimated the unconditioned character of divine love. And in a most unreflective way Paul may have been attuned favorably to these. Perhaps in a moment of reflection on the God proclaimed by the followers of Jesus, Paul suddenly felt the congruity between their dramatic accounts and the repressed elements of his own sentient consciousness. His conversion, then, took the form of a sudden flooding into harmony of the various levels of his world-involvement. In Christianity he found the story that best expressed his deepest feelings. Sentient consciousness could now have a story commensurate with it. The freedom that Paul experienced can be expressed partially in terms of his liberation from the "cover-story" of fanatical Pharisaism designed both to give his life meaning and to mask deep-felt requirements of his soul. Adherence to such a cover-story in self-deception involves as we know from modern psychology the desperate diffusion of one's energy to fuel the elements of combat and conflict within oneself. It seems quite feasible to suppose that the psychic aspect of Paul's liberating transformation involved a release from a conflict between the sentient and narrative modes of his being. And, with this, the psychic energy previously diverted to the warding off of internal challenges by sentient to narrative consciousness is now smoothly integrated into the incomparably dynamic and vital relations Paul established with the world around him.

Paul's writing clearly illustrates the feeling that follows the release from a life in which spontaneities are repressed and one is lived heteronomously by a "law" outside of oneself, whether this "law" is introjected into consciousness or remains situated in the outer forum.

There are innumerable other examples we could have provided to illustrate how a religiously narrative revision may promote the process of appropriating and coinciding with one's basic spontaneities. The one we have provided is not by any means intended to be the only illustration of our point. What I would emphasize again, however, is that self-deception cannot be vanquished by theory alone. Acceptance of self always requires some (not necessarily articulated) immersion in a story in which the whole self can be reshaped. Philosophy can only point the way toward those dramatic incarnations of life that are indispensable to this process. It is not a substitute for them.

Prior to an immersion in the religiously narrative and interpersonal atmosphere of being accepted unconditionally, we can conclude, it may be most difficult for anyone to look deeply into himself. Intellectual powers simply will not suffice. Rather they will be used to rationalize a state of self-deception. What makes psychoanalysis successful, when it is so, is the environing mood of acceptance that the therapist radiates in the therapeutic encounter and that permits the patient to express the feelings and desires which have been previously buried due to their social unacceptability. Similarly what makes a religious story, such as that of God's unconditional love, a story which promotes the quest for truthfulness toward oneself, is the narrative "world" that it constitutes in such a way as to eliminate any fear of uncovering one's darker side. One is accepted in any case. Nothing that he can do or leave undone will change this basic situation. There is no longer any need to hide from oneself. One can now accept his past, link up to his previously repressed experiences and live fully in the present. In accepting himself as he is, he is free in a genuinely human meaning of the term. The only barrier to such freedom is the refusal to accept the fact that one is accepted. And this refusal is rooted in the will to power and the desire for mastery.

The desire to know is fully liberated, it seems to me, only in the spontaneous act of entrusting one's life to a story embodying such unconditional acceptance. The quest for truth requires the quest for such a story.

Conclusion

> The restlessness of the human spirit makes the prospect of life opening up before one all the way to death seem monotonous. The only cure for the restlessness, it seems, is consent, a Yes to the life of the spirit, a Yes to the restlessness itself. The restlessness is like the unquiet of the sea, the constant motion of the waves. To be willingly unquiet is to be quiet. It is like a calm in which the sea becomes transparent to its depth.[1]

These words aptly represent the state of self-acceptance that we have held to be the goal of philosophy. The root of human restlessness we have called the desire to know. And the business of the philosopher we have held to be that of promoting a continually more vigorous Yes to the imperatives of the mind that forever stir us toward further questioning.

Stating that this is a goal is one thing. Achieving it is another. So philosophy cannot be indifferent to the question of how such an ideal of self-acceptance can be translated from paper to actual achievement. It must be attentive to whatever concrete constituents of human life might inspire the Yes to the restlessness whose goal is the unrestricted realm of the intelligible and the real. Self-affirmation cannot be brought about as long as consciousness remains isolated in the theoretic pattern (as our own reflections have been). Theory is of itself impotent to engender the fully personal act of surrender to the dynamic source of self-transcendence that leads us toward further questions and shifts of horizon. The most that theoretical, philosophical insight can do (and it is here that philosophy achieves its greatest success) is to point the way back to life. A great deal is gained by the turn to theory, but it is lost if we attempt to subdue our indomitable restlessness by making theory itself the goal of the spirit's striving. The absolutizing instinct of which both psychotherapists and theologians speak is particularly

174

prone to making us think that once we have entrapped our world in the reticulations of systematic thought we have mastered it. By capitulating to this instinct for idolatry we turn away from the mind's basic imperative, "be open," with its requirement that our world be mediated also through primal fields of meaning and through the spontaneous activity of living sentiently, interpersonally, narratively and aesthetically.

What our own theoretical approach has led us to, then, is the recognition that theory is not enough for genuine living. It is not alone capable of bringing about the vital act of self-acceptance that is a prerequisite of commitment to the pursuit of truth. What theory can do is humbly recognize the necessity of primal, narrative involvement as a condition for achieving the restful peace that follows from the Yes to one's restlessness. Self-appropriation requires also active participation in some story, one that itself is open to the revisions demanded by the quietless desire to know, and one that arouses a sense of gratitude as the response to one's creatureliness.

If the philosopher's task is that of finding ways of bringing about the Yes to his own desire to know he is obliged to ask among other things how stories of God might relate to this endeavor. In Chapter III we concluded that the image of God as Creator intends to motivate believers to a grateful acceptance of their being in spite of the restlessness that continually exposes the poverty of what they have achieved in the various quests of their lives. Without a sense of gratitude, our restlessness becomes a torment. It becomes filled with a hunger for power, with resentment or indifference, and the Yes to oneself never fully comes forth. By awakening a sense of gratitude, however, religious imagery fulfills our fundamental criterion of truth, fidelity to the desire to know, by keeping in view the element of unrestrictedness, the recondite awareness of which is the source of our restlessness. And (as argued in Chapter VII) in the image of a God of unconditional acceptance of man, a God of redemptive love who befriends man, it is possible for one to have the narrative context for the removal of self-deception. Participation in the story of the Yes by God to man on the basis of friendship rather than coercion provides for many the symbolic basis for a sincere Yes to themselves. This act of self-acceptance in religious conversion is not separable from the Yes to self that is the goal of any authentic philosophy, even though philosophy is not able to bring about the affirmation all by itself. Religious self-acceptance may very well be a necessary *de facto* condition for a lively appropriation of the mind's imperatives, and in a special way when these imperatives issue the Socratic "know thyself."

At this point we may bring forth two questions that, assuredly, many readers have been asking all along. First, have we not implicitly subordinated religion to philosophy in our asking whether the former serves the goal of self-knowledge toward which the philosopher aspires? And, second, precisely what is to be gained by the Yes to my desire to know and the imperatives that continually impel consciousness forward toward no definite point of rest? We shall discuss each of these in turn.

The first of these two overlapping questions asks whether we have not made religion the handmaiden of philosophy. Have we not perhaps performed a Hegelian-like sublation of religion by reason? I think not. I have maintained that the religious act originates spontaneously, independently of any theoretical control. But I have not argued that this spontaneous religious act is to be abrogated by or absorbed into the systematic structure of a philosophy. On the contrary, I have held that at the end of his reflections the philosopher is obliged to turn us back (perhaps in a different way) toward the pretheoretical, narrative and symbolic modes of being that alone can provide humans with the depth of meaning necessary to sustain their interest and vitality. The goal of self-acceptance can be pointed to and partially clarified by theory, but it can only be *achieved* in a nonreflective, partially self-forgetful act of spontaneous immersion in the narrative mode. So in this sense philosophy does not lead us beyond religion but back to it, ideally with an attitude of renewed reverence and appreciation for its symbolic depth.

Second, we must ask again what benefits might result from the self-appropriation toward which we have directed our study. Does not the Yes to one's restlessness promise only more restlessness? How can we say that the act of coinciding with the imperatives of the mind can bring peace and freedom?

In its infancy our striving is hardly aware of the imperatives. As we grow, however, we experience them at first dimly, then more intensely and perhaps eventually we advert to them in the reflective manner we have followed in this book. At first these precepts have an extrinsic, heteronomous quality to them. We are, from the start, quite attentive and partially intelligent, but the imperatives to be reflective and responsible are not so easily allowed to come to the center of consciousness. As we ascend through the four levels of consciousness (experience, understanding, judgment and decision) we find that their corresponding imperatives may appear increasingly extrinsic to the inclinations of the moment. And it is only gradually, and never totally, that we accept the imperatives as the center of our selfhood. The temptation to escape from the inescapable is never totally overcome.

As the philosopher seeks for ways by which he may more fully endorse the exigencies of the mind in an intimately personal way, he encounters among other things the stories and exercises presented by the world's religious traditions. If, for him, the mind is reducible to "seeing" or taking a good look, then he will dismiss as nonsense any religious talk about the unseen, the sacred or the absolute, about creation and redemption. If, however, the mind to whose imperatives he wants to be faithful is experienced, understood and accepted as dynamic, open-ended, intelligent, critical and responsible then he may not want to overlook the value of religious commitment in sustaining the unrestricted, measureless depth in which alone such a mind can live.

A person will withhold the Yes to his restlessness when it seems to lead toward an abyss that holds only more struggle, pain, endless and meaningless transition. It is only when the abyss turns into a ground that his restlessness seems to have a purpose. Then what was sheer, terrifying depth without measure becomes the source of joy. Paul Tillich writes at the end of his sermon on the "Depth of Existence":

The end of the way is joy. And joy is deeper than suffering. It is ultimate. Let me express this in the words of a man who, in passionate striving for the depth, was caught by destructive forces and did not know the word to conquer them. Friedrich

Nietzsche writes: "The world is deep, and deeper than the day could read. Deep is its woe. Joy deeper still than grief can be. Woe says: Hence, go! But joys want all eternity, want deep, profound eternity."

Eternal joy is the end of the ways of God. This is the message of all religions. The Kingdom of God is peace and joy. This is the message of Christianity. But eternal joy is not to be reached by living on the surface. It is rather attained by breaking through the surface, by penetrating the deep things of ourselves, of our world, and of God. The moment in which we reach the last depth of our lives is the moment in which we can experience the joy that has eternity within it, the hope that cannot be destroyed, and the truth on which life and death are built. For in the depth is truth; and in the depth is hope; and in the depth is joy.[2]

Without such a promise of joy as that which religions provide, the theoretician will find it most difficult to put us in touch with our striving for depth in our existence. He must seek for the words, the symbols, the stories that portray the depth as not only abyss but also as ground. By naming with symbols of joy the depth toward which our restlessness penetrates, religious language gives man the courage to affirm his striving without resentment at the fact that he never comes to a point of final immobility.

I have argued in this book that it is possible for us first to tolerate and then to embrace our restlessness only when we move back from theory into such a religiously narrative mode of involvement.

NOTES

INTRODUCTION

1. Mircea Eliade, *Patterns in . Comparative Religion*, trans. by Rosemary Sheed (New York: Sheed and Ward, 1958), p. xiii.

2. Paul Ricoeur, *Fallible Man*, trans. by Charles Kelbley (Chicago: Henry Regnery Co., 1967), p. 8 f.

3. Henry Duméry, *Faith and Reflection*, ed. by Louis Dupré, trans. by S. McNierney and M. B. Murphy, R.S.H.M. (New York: Herder and Herder, 1968), p. 71 f.

4. *Ibid.*, p. 76.

5. Paul Ricoeur, *The Symbolism of Evil*, trans. by E. Buchanan (Boston: Beacon Press, 1967), p. 350.

6. *Ibid.*, p. 349.

I
IDENTIFYING THE DESIRE TO KNOW

1. Cf. Langdon Gilkey, *Naming the Whirlwind: The Renewal of God-Language* (Indianapolis and New York: Bobbs-Merrill Co., Inc., 1969).

2. Bernard Lonergan, S.J., *Insight: A Study of Human Understanding*, 3rd ed. (New York: Philosophical Library, 1970), p. 283.

3. Kent Bach, *Exit-Existentialism* (Belmont, California: Wadsworth Publishing Co., 1973), p. 4.

4. Alfred North Whitehead, *Process and Reality* (New York: Macmillan-Free Press, 1969), p. 303.

5. W. T. Stace, "Man against Darkness," in Frederick J. Streng *et al.*, *Ways of Being Religious* (Englewood Cliffs, N.J.: Prentice Hall, Inc., 1973), p. 341.

6. Mircea Eliade, *Myth and Reality*, trans. by W. R. Trask (New York: Harper & Row, 1963), p. 139.

7. Following Bernard Lonergan's approach to method in *Method in Theology* (New York: Herder and Herder, 1972).

8. Lonergan, *Insight*, especially pp. 271-347.

9. The following is an adaptation of Lonergan's cognitional theory fully elaborated in *Insight*.

10. Lonergan, *Insight*, pp. 396 ff.

11. *Ibid.*, p. 335 f.

12. Cf. Lonergan, *Method in Theology*, p. 18.

13. Bernard Lonergan, S.J., "Cognitional Structure," in F. E. Crowe, S.J., ed., *Collection* (New York: Herder and Herder, 1967), pp. 221-39.

14. Henry Duméry, *The Problem of God*, trans. by Charles Courtney (Northwestern University Press, 1964), p. 7.

15. *Ibid.*, p. 25.

16. Cf. Lonergan, *Insight*, pp. xviii, 4, 9 and *passim*.

17. See, however, Michael Novak's important work, *Belief and Unbelief* (New York: The Macmillan Co., 1965).

18. *Nicomachean Ethics* I, 1, 1094a, 1-4, in Richard McKeon, *The Basic Works of Aristotle* (New York: Random House, 1941).

II
RELIGION AND THE ELEMENTS OF CONSCIOUSNESS

1. Lonergan, *Insight*, pp. 220-22, 348-50, 636-39 and *passim*.

2. Søren Kierkegaard, *The Sickness Unto Death*, trans. by Walter Lowrie (Garden City, N.Y.: Doubleday Anchor Books, 1954), p. 175 f.

3. Lonergan, *Insight*, pp. 350-52, 636-39.

4. Cf. Wilfred Cantwell Smith, "On the Comparative Study of Re-

ligion," in Walter H. Capps, ed., *Ways of Understanding Religion* (New York: The Macmillan Co., 1972), pp. 190-203.

5. Cf. Richard Comstock *et al.*, *Religion and Man: An Introduction* (New York: Harper & Row, 1971), pp. 21-27.

6. Rudolf Otto, *The Idea of the Holy*, 2nd ed., trans. by John W. Harvey (New York: Oxford University Press, 1950), pp. 5-7.

7. Eliade, *Patterns in Comparative Religion*, pp. 12-14, 29 f.

8. Otto, *The Idea of the Holy*, pp. 8-11.

9. A clear, concise statement of Tillich's view of religion may be found in his *Theology of Culture* (New York: Oxford University Press, 1959), pp. 3-9.

10. Paul Tillich, *The Courage to Be* (New Haven: Yale University Press, 1952), p. 164.

11. Plato, *Symposium*, 200.

12. Aristotle, *Nicomachean Ethics* X, 1174a and b.

13. Paul Ricoeur, *Fallible Man*, p. 140.

14. *Ibid.*, p. 142.

15. *Ibid.*, p. 105.

16. *Ibid.*

17. The following scheme is to some extent patterned on one given by Calvin Schrag, "Ontology and the Possibility of Religious Knowledge," *Journal of Religion*, XLII (1962), 87-94. However, I have considerably modified it, especially by introducing the "narrative" mode where Schrag speaks of the "historic."

18. F. D. Schleiermacher, *On Religion*, trans. by John Oman (New York: Harper & Row, 1958).

19. Martin Heidegger, *Sein und Zeit*, 7th ed. (Tübingen: Max Neimeyer Verlag, 1953), p. 120.

20. Stephen Crites, "The Narrative Quality of Experience," *Journal of the American Academy of Religion*, XXXIX (1971), 291-311.

21. *Ibid.*

22. I am here indebted to an excellent discussion of the question of religion and art by Louis Dupré, *The Other Dimension* (Garden City, N.Y.: Doubleday & Co., 1972), pp. 228-42.

23. Susanne Langer, *Feeling and Form* (New York: Charles Scribner's Sons, 1953), pp. 69-279.

III
RELIGION AND PSYCHIC STRIVING

1. See, for example, Frederick Perls, Ralph E. Hefferline, and Paul Goodman, *Gestalt Therapy* (New York: Delta Books, 1957), p. 363.

2. Sigmund Freud, *The Future of an Illusion*, trans. by W. D. Robson-Scott; revised and newly edited by James Strachey (Garden City, N.Y.: Doubleday Anchor Books, 1964).

3. Abraham Maslow, "The Need to Know and the Fear of Knowing," in David Lester, ed., *Explorations in Exploration* (New York: Van Nostrand-Reinhold Co., 1969), pp. 199-217.

4. Freud, *The Future of an Illusion*, pp. 69-73.

5. Sigmund Freud, *Beyond the Pleasure Principle*, trans. by James Strachey (New York: Bantam Books, 1959), pp. 21, 26 f., 42, 64, 108.

6. Sigmund Freud, *Civilization and Its Discontents*, trans. by James Strachey (New York: W. W. Norton & Co., 1962), p. 24.

7. Sigmund Freud, *A General Introduction to Psychoanalysis*, trans. by Joan Riviere (New York: Pocket Books, 1952), p. 381.

8. Freud, *The Future of an Illusion*, p. 92.

9. Jacques Monod, *Chance and Necessity*, trans. by Austryn Wainhouse (New York: Vintage Books, 1972), p. 176.

10. Perhaps the best discussion of the personal coefficient in scientific knowing is that of Michael Polanyi, *Personal Knowledge* (New York: Harper Torchbooks, 1964).

11. Lonergan, *Insight*, pp. 191-206.

12. Tillich, *The Courage to Be*, pp. 75-76.

13. Lonergan, *Insight*, pp. 636-39.

14. *Ibid.*

15. Hannah Arendt, *The Human Condition* (Chicago: University of Chicago Press, 1958), p. 302.

16. Ernest Becker, *The Denial of Death* (New York: The Free Press, 1973).

17. *Ibid.*, p. 189.

18. *Ibid.*, p. 188 f.

19. *Ibid.*, p. 189.

20. *Ibid.*, p. 199.

21. *Ibid.*

22. W. T. Stace, in Streng, *Ways of Being Religious*, p. 342.

IV
RELIGION AND THE DESIRE FOR MEANING

1. Herbert Fingarette, *The Self in Transformation* (New York: Harper & Row, 1965).

2. Albert Camus, *The Myth of Sisyphus and Other Essays*, trans. by J. O'Brien (New York: Vintage Books, 1955), p. 4.

3. For the following summary cf. Peter Berger, *The Sacred Canopy* (Garden City, N.Y.: Doubleday & Co., 1969).

4. *Ibid.*, pp. 81-101.

5. C. G. Jung, *The Archetypes and the Collective Unconscious* (*Collected Works*, Vol. 9, I), trans. by R. F. C. Hull (New York: Pantheon Books, 1959), pp. 3-53.

6. C. G. Jung, *Two Essays on Analytical Psychology*, 2nd ed. (*Col-

lected Works, Vol. 7), trans. by R. F. C. Hull (New York: Pantheon Books, 1966), pp. 163, 166-68, 283 f.

7. Erich Fromm, *Escape From Freedom* (New York: Avon Books, 1965), and Paul Tillich, *The Courage to Be*, p. 49.

8. Michael Novak, *The Experience of Nothingness* (New York: Harper Colophon Books, 1971), p. 17 f.

9. Becker, *The Denial of Death*, p. 56.

10. Cf. John Dunne, *The Way of All the Earth* (New York: The Macmillan Co., 1972), pp. i, 154, 157 and *passim*.

11. Kierkegaard, *The Sickness Unto Death*, pp. 163 ff.

12. Cf. Ray Hart, *Unfinished Man and the Imagination* (New York: Herder and Herder, 1968), pp. 198 ff.

13. Cf. Eulalio Baltazar, *God Within Process* (Paramus: Newman Press, 1970), pp. 17 ff.

V
THE PROBLEM OF GOD-LANGUAGE

1. Assertive language is understood here as language that pictures or points to some object. Certain forms of traditional theology as well as numerous contemporary critics of religion simply assume that religious and theological utterance intend some (hidden) object. It is this objectifying conception of religious discourse that renders it so problematic. We shall contend that the problem of the meaning of religious language arises partly because it is so difficult to shake the conviction that all meaningful language must be objective, in the sense of pointing to something "out there" totally detached from the subject.

2. Cf. T. Patrick Burke, *The Reluctant Vision* (Philadelphia: Fortress Press, 1974), p. 13.

3. R. B. Braithwaite, *An Empiricist's View of the Nature of Religious Belief* (Cambridge: Cambridge University Press, 1955), p. 19.

4. Frederick Ferré, *Language, Logic and God* (New York: Harper Torchbooks, 1969), pp. 8-17 and 58-66.

5. The "verification principle" has had many formulations and we are discussing only one facet of it here. For further elaboration cf. Ferré, pp. 12-17.

6. Ludwig Wittgenstein, *Tractatus Logico-Philosophicus* (London: Routledge and Kegan Paul, 1922).

7. Bertrand Russell, *An Inquiry into Truth and Meaning* (London: George Allen and Unwin, Ltd., 1940).

8. A. J. Ayer, *Language, Truth and Logic* (New York: Dover Publications, n.d.), p. 115.

9. *Ibid.*

10. Cf. Ferré, pp. 16, 32-34, 50-53.

11. *Ibid.*, p. 61.

12. On the Wittgensteinian notion of "language games" cf. Edward Cell, *Language, Existence and God* (Nashville: Abingdon Press, 1971), pp. 141-211.

13. Cf. Ferré, p. 63 f.

14. Ayer, p. 68.

15. This aspect of meaning is most clearly expressed in the writings of Bernard Lonergan. I am indebted to him for a great deal of what follows, especially my discussion of horizon and conversion. I do not thereby imply that my treatment is in every respect in agreement with his, only that I have found it valuable for my approach to the problem of the meaning of religious language. Cf. especially *Method in Theology*, pp. 57-99.

16. For a lucid introduction to this most important exercise I enthusiastically refer the reader again to Michael Novak's *Belief and Unbelief.*

17. For a discussion of the various realms of meaning, cf. Lonergan, *Method in Theology*, pp. 81-85.

18. Cf. Lonergan, *Method in Theology*, pp. 235-44.

19. For this way of putting the question I am indebted especially to

Emerich Coreth's *Metaphysics*, ed. and trans. by Joseph Donceel (New York: Herder and Herder, 1968), pp. 45 ff.

20. Cf. Novak, pp. 56-57.

21. This term is Lonergan's. See *Method in Theology*, p. 238.

22. Lonergan, *Insight*, p. 320 f.

23. Paul Tillich, *The Shaking of the Foundations* (New York: Charles Scribner's Sons, 1948), p. 55.

24. See the discussion of Lonergan's notion of conversion by Bernard Tyrrell, *Bernard Lonergan's Philosophy of God* (Notre Dame: University of Notre Dame Press, 1974), pp. 33-68.

VI
BELIEF IN GOD AND THE DESIRE TO KNOW

1. Cf. Hart, *Unfinished Man and the Imagination*, pp. 116, 205 ff.

2. Camus, *The Myth of Sisyphus*, p. 38.

3. *Ibid.*, pp. 24 ff.

4. Colin Wilson, *The Outsider* (Boston: Houghton Mifflin Co., 1956), p. 120.

5. Charles E. Winquist, "The Act of Storytelling and the Self's homecoming," *Journal of the American Academy of Religion*, XLII (1974), 101.

6. Jean-Paul Sartre, *Nausea*, trans. by L. Alexander (New York: New Directions Pub. Corp., 1964), p. 33.

7. *Ibid.*, p. 40.

8. Joseph Campbell, *The Hero with a Thousand Faces*, 2nd ed. (Princeton, N.J.: Princeton University Press, 1968), p. 30.

9. Peter Berger, *A Rumor of Angels* (Garden City, N.Y.: Doubleday Anchor Books, 1970), p. 53.

10. Tillich, *The Courage to Be*, p. 81.

11. *Ibid.*, p. 177.

12. Examples of this are Karl Barth, *Church Dogmatics* II, part 1, trans. by T.H.L. Parker, *et al.* (Edinburgh: T. & T. Clark, 1957), pp. 3-178; and Martin Buber, *I and Thou*, 2nd ed., trans. by Ronald Gregor Smith (New York: Charles Scribner's Sons, 1958).

13. Duméry, *The Problem of God*, p. 57.

14. Cf. Lonergan, *Insight,* pp. 53-54, 478 ff., 685, 380-81, and *passim.*

15. Cf. Emerich Coreth, *Metaphysics*, pp. 17-44.

16. Milton K. Munitz, *The Mystery of Existence* (New York: Appleton-Century-Crofts, 1965), p. 61.

17. *Ibid.*, p. 69.

18. Lonergan, *Insight*, p. 652.

19. Cf. Bernard Tyrell, *Bernard Lonergan's Philosophy of God*, pp. 61 ff.

20. Karl Jaspers, *Philosophical Faith and Revelation*, trans. by E. B. Ashton (New York: Harper & Row, 1967), p. 84.

VII
RELIGIOUS STORY AND SELF-ACCEPTANCE

1. Herbert Fingarette, *Self-Deception* (London: Routledge and Kegan Paul, 1969), p. 1.

2. *Ibid.*, p. 139 f.

3. *Ibid.*, pp. 144 ff.

4. Leslie Farber, "Perfectibility and the Psychoanalytic Candidate," partially reprinted in William Lynch, *Images of Hope* (Notre Dame: University of Notre Dame Press, 1965), p. 269 f.

5. Cf. Daniel Yankelovich and William Barrett, *Ego and Instinct* (New York: Vintage Books, 1971), pp. 172, 282, 325, 423.

6. On the notion of the "absolutizing instinct" see Lynch, *Images of Hope*, pp. 105-25.

7. Cf. especially Ricoeur, *The Symbolism of Evil*, pp. 161-305.

8. Jean-Paul Sartre, *Being and Nothingness*, trans. by Hazel E. Barnes (New York: Philosophical Library, 1956), pp. 553-56.

9. Ricoeur, *The Symbolism of Evil*, p. 258.

10. Cf. Jean-Paul Sartre, *Existentialism*, trans. by Bernard Frechtman (New York: Philosophical Library, 1947).

11. This is clearly implied in Sartre's defense of his position in *Existentialism*.

12. E.g. Sartre, *Existentialism*, p. 55.

13. This is especially true of the so-called "existential" approach to psychoanalysis; e.g., Rollo May *et al.*, eds., *Existence* (New York: Simon and Schuster, 1958).

14. Fingarette, *Self-Deception*, p. 47 f.

15. *Ibid.*, p. 50.

16. Cf. Sam Keen, *To a Dancing God* (New York: Harper & Row, 1970), p. 130.

17. I have borrowed this expression from Paul Tillich, *The Courage to Be*, pp. 182 ff., but I am using it in a slightly different sense from that intended by Tillich.

18. Paul Tillich, *Systematic Theology*, I (Chicago: University of Chicago Press, 1951), p. 245.

19. Henry Duméry, *The Problem of God*, p. 119.

20. Henry Duméry, *Philosophie de la religion*, I (Paris: Presses Universitaires de France, 1957), p. 70, cited in R. F. de Brabander, *Religion and Human Autonomy* (The Hague: Martinus Nijhoff, 1972), p. 119.

21. Henry Duméry, *The Problem of God*, p. 119 n.

22. Cf. Raimundo Panikkar, *The Trinity and the Religious Experience of Man* (New York: Orbis Books, 1973), p. 46 f.

23. Raymond Panikkar, "Nirvana and the Awareness of the Absolute," in Joseph P. Whelan, S.J., ed., *The God-Experience* (Paramus, N.J.: Newman Press, 1971), p. 96.

24. Cf. Panikkar, *The Trinity and the Religious Experience of Man.*

25. Keen, *To a Dancing God*, p. 135 f.

26. *Ibid.*, p. 136.

27. Alfred North Whitehead, *Religion in the Making* (New York: The Macmillan Co., 1926, 1960), p. 16.

CONCLUSION

1. John Dunne, *Time and Myth* (Garden City, N.Y.: Doubleday & Co., 1973), p. 79.

2. Paul Tillich, *The Shaking of the Foundations* (New York: Charles Scribner's Sons, 1948), p. 63.